Make Believe:
Discovering and Creating Magical Experiences

D. Michael Smith

"*Make Believe* is overwhelming . . . a magical wonder."
Robert E. Neale, Ph.D., author of *An Essay on Magic*

Make Believe:
Discovering and Creating Magical Experiences

"I submit that magic is the theater of magical imagination. . . . It is a display of the impossible as the working of the imagination, which fosters make-believe."
Robert E. Neale

"Indeed, most people come to a magic show wanting to *make believe* and *play* with our impossible things."
Lawrence Hass

"The world is full of magic things, patiently waiting for our senses to grow sharper."
W. B. Yeats

"What is this 'experience of magic'? . . . The answer is obvious: I can avoid this question simply by narrowing the focus of my magical interest to merely how tricks work. If we so narrow our focus, it is easy indeed to avoid all the basic questions in magic—and in life!"
Eugene Burger

"Magic is created when imagination touches reality."
George Parker

What Others Are Saying about
Make Believe: Discovering and Creating Magical Experiences

"*Make Believe* is a magical cornucopia of pieces that produce dazzling stimulations about magic. The author is a magician whose make believe engages our imaginations. So read the book, the entire book. But don't stop there. Reread the pieces that are wonders for you."

Robert E. Neale, Ph.D.
Philosopher, author, teacher, creator

Mike Smith's book *Make Believe* will delight any magician who thinks about our craft. His essays are therapeutic and inspiring—they remind us there is so much more to magic and magic performance, than tricks and cons, jokes and pointless patter. Then Mike "walks the walk" by sharing three fully developed presentations of his own. Highly recommended!

Lawrence Hass, Ph.D.
Dean of the McBride Magic & Mystery School

Mike . . . has the ability to take sometimes complex and arcane concepts in magical thinking and turn them into easy-to-understand, thought provoking topics of study, and more importantly, conversations.

. . . his insights and conversational tone make sometimes dry and academic topics of the psychology of magic and performing entertaining and engaging—and that's a testament to his skill in conveying these ideas. If you want to give your performance more focus, intent, creativity, and impact, this is the book for you."

Pix Smith
Founding Director of the Dallas Puppet Theatre

"Mike's deep respect for the art of magic combined with a love of acting is refreshing. By integrating theatrical techniques he truly believes a performance can be elevated. Magicians and actors are both performers. So then what can magicians learn from an actor? What can actors learn from a magician? Mike believes training classically and improving improvisation skills can only benefit a performer."

Maggie Younkin
Education Associate and Training Artist, Theatre Arlington, Texas

"Michael has written this thoroughly entertaining book that incorporates the science of magic and the art of illusions. The book not only reinforces important principles found in neuroscience and other areas of psychology, but it is also a good, fun read if you just want to learn how to perform magic."

Patricia Lyons, Ph.D.
Psychology Professor, Mountain View College, Dallas, Texas

Make Believe:
Discovering and Creating Magical Experiences

D. Michael Smith

Make Believe: Discovering and Creating Magical Experiences
D. Michael Smith

First Published in 2020

Cover image: ©
Cover and interior design: Jennifer McGuire
Interior Photos: D. Michael Smith
Back Cover photo: David Clanton
Copy-Editing: Geoff Grimes, Lawrence Hass

ISBN-13: 978-1-7334722-1-0

This book is dedicated to my wife, Phyllis, the creator of incredible magical experiences in my life.

I want to thank the following individuals and groups for the inspiration, encouragement and support in my interest in magic and the writing of *Make Believe:*

Geoff Grimes, very good friend and fellow traveler in discovering and creating magical experiences;

Larry Hass, friend, teacher, editor, and Dean of the McBride Magic & Mystery School;

Dal Sanders, The Society of American Magicians, Past National President, and friend;

Members and participants of the Dallas Magic Clubs, the Fort Worth Magicians Club, and the Mid-Cities Magic Circle;

Staff and participants of the McBride Magic & Mystery School's "Magic and Meaning Conference;"

Mark Wilson and Nani Darnell, who introduced this eleven-year-old boy to the world of make believe, wonder, and magic;

and my family—Phyllis, Jennifer, Elon, Amy, Chad, and especially to our grandchildren—Abby, Nick, Ramona, and Isaac.

Contents

Before Words
Dal Sanders

I have enjoyed watching Mike Smith write this book. It has been a true pleasure watching it take shape, word by word and chapter by chapter. Much of it I got to read before anyone else because most of it was originally part of Mike's monthly column in *The Wizard's Scroll*, the newsletter of The Dallas Magic Club.

When I became "the Scribe of The Scroll" (aka the editor), Mike was the President of The Dallas Magic Club. I had always enjoyed reading the thoughts of the Presidents of other magic clubs so I asked Mike if he would be interested in a "President's Column" for our newsletter. I was confident that he would do a really good job; I had seen his creativity before.

Mike had presented a series of mini-lectures for the magic club on the Psychology and Philosophy of The Art of Magic. It was fascinating. His presentations were informative, well researched and best of all . . . he was NOT boring. You read that right, Mike delivered lectures about magic's psychology and philosophy that were interesting and fun. At the end of the lecture he would pass out a written copy of his mini-lecture. After reading what he wrote I thought that he should share his written thoughts in our newsletter.

Mike was a psychotherapist and family counselor throughout his career. Recently he retired as the Senior Pastoral Counselor at the Pastoral Counseling Center in Dallas where he advised and assessed interns applying for credentialing as family therapists and professional counselors. Mike also has a strong background in theater. In fact, we would often bump into each other at a play, musical or other performance around Dallas.

After Mike's term as President of the Dallas Magic Club was over, I asked him to stay on and write a monthly column for The Scroll. He agreed and over the past eight years he has shared his thoughts, his philosophy and his passion for the Art of Magic with the members of our club. Now, you get to read it and enjoy it too . . . still, I get to brag that I read it first.

Dal Sanders

Dal Sanders, M.I.M.C., With Gold Star
The Society of American Magicians,
Past National President
The Wizard's Scroll, Editor

D. Michael Smith

Foreword

Geoffrey Grimes, Ph.D.

Michael "Mike" Smith is known in the North Texas magic community affectionately as "Dr. Mike." A retired family therapist, Mike served for many years as the Senior Pastoral Counselor for the Pastoral Counseling Center in Dallas, the largest counselling center in North Texas. Mike holds a B. A. Degree in Psychology from the University of Houston as well as two Master's Degrees—one in Divinity and another in Pastoral Care and Counseling—both from Southwestern Theological Seminary and Brite Divinity School, Texas Christian University in Fort Worth. Additionally, Mike also is an ordained pastor. This complementary academic/social services background helps frame his approach to magic, an avocation since his boyhood days in Tyler, Texas, when he happened on to a young magician, Mark Wilson, and his wife, Nani Darnell, who were performing for the opening of a grocery store.

Mike's professional career in counseling stretches across the United States, but it has been in North Texas where his enthusiasm for magic has been nurtured. He is one of the very few who have served as president of both the Fort Worth Magicians Club and the Dallas Magic Clubs, Inc., a testimony to the respect his magic holds for his North Texas compeers.

Today, Mike performs for parlor, stage, and restaurant arenas. For the past several years he has performed weekly at a Dallas restaurant, but also entertains in libraries, schools, churches, and other adult venues. Most recently, Mike has developed a magical lecture on perception, drawing upon his resources from psychology to address the ways that magicians rely on sense perception to create the illusions so identified with the magical entertainer. The lecture, "Now You See Me, Now You . . .?" he delivers to college and university students in Introduction to Psychology classes.

Mike's essays contained in this small volume reflect his keen insights into magical performance and the relationships that magicians create with their audiences. Widely read, he draws upon the works of authors, magical performers, theatrical directors, actors, philosophers, psychologists,

3

playwrights, and visual artists, pulling from their works threads of truths and insights that he hopes will give thought to each of us as we consider our own approaches to the craft and art that is magical entertainment.

At the same time, the *genre* Mike has chosen to communicate these insights—the short essay—complements the growing digital culture immersed in quick sound bites, blogs, and bullet points. Each essay can easily be read and digested in a single sitting. The tone of each piece is relaxed, personable, and always encouraging. However, each is a serious, heartfelt appeal to all of us to strive to make our performance pieces *truly magical* rather than merely entertaining for audiences who often bring to the experience of our magic popular and quite prominent preconceptions that belie magic as serious art.

In other words, behind Mike's enthusiasm and passion is the realization of the place that magic plays in the lives of everyone. Mike's own "magical world view" has been deeply influenced by the works of Robert E. Neale who, in his *An Essay on Magic,* has characterized stage magic as only a narrow corridor in the broad arena of what he calls "Life Magic." Neale's works are disturbing, sometimes even shocking to those of us who think of magic as only casual entertainment. Mike gladly acknowledges, as well, the influence of the late Eugene Burger, beloved throughout the magical universe as both a master teacher as well as iconic performer. And, practicing what he "preaches," Mike is a seasoned student of theater, returning in his retirement to acting classes that were the focus of his early college years before he migrated into the fields of philosophy, theology, and psychology. A dominant theme running throughout his essays is the relationship between magical performance and the theater and the magician's acceptance of himself as "an actor"—in the literal sense of its meaning—"playing the part of a magician."

Finally, I would be remiss if I didn't add a personal note to these introductory remarks. In the context of a warm and complementary friendship, we share much in common in the world of magical entertainment, in our commitment to it as performers in bettering ourselves for our audiences, and in the mutual realization of our role as senior citizens in our magical communities. First, Mike and I live in the same small city of DeSoto in Southwest Dallas County, Texas, a factor that means we can get together in our magical ventures quite regularly, and we do. We enjoy many informal meetings in which we discuss magic and magical performance. Out of these discussions we have developed several different shows that we have presented in libraries, public schools, colleges, and local restaurants.

That proximity has also made it convenient to take on substantially larger projects, including a two-year enterprise in which we indexed major themes in the works of Robert "Bob" Neale. Our mutual fascination with the human behavior of magic—its practice and performance—has led us to the annual McBride Mystery School's "Magic and Meaning" conferences hosted each fall in Las Vegas, a venue that has opened up relationships with fellow performers and thinkers on the magical arts from around the world.

And the realization and acceptance of our age as septuagenarians has made our work together even more poignant, given the factors of our health and station in life. Not without histories of various health issues, we both remain active in leadership roles in our communities and in the two major magic organizations in Dallas and Fort Worth.

This small collection of essays represents our latest project, what, at one level, is just another excuse we have created to justify getting together again—what's any good project for? But it is also a serious attempt to create a portal through which we hope to stimulate a dialogue among our peers, and to document, in a more permanent way, key ideas, principles, and practices about the magical art as we have experienced it in our small North Texas circle of magical entertainment. Mike's essays enclosed herein bristle with insight and should prove engaging to any one of us interested in better understanding principles of good performance and our own behavior in this niche corridor of human experience.

D. Michael Smith

Introduction

Little did I know that when Dal Sanders, editor of the Dallas Magic Clubs electronic newsletter, *The Wizard's Scroll*, asked me to write a column in 2012 that I would still be writing the column after fifty plus installations. The column has been a journey for me and has involved some changes along the way.

I began writing the columns to focus on the psychology of deception for magicians. Dal asked me to write these columns after I made several brief lectures on the psychology of deception for the Dallas Magic Clubs meetings. In January 2018 I changed the subtitle for the series from "BeLIEve Me, But Cut the Cards: A Psychology of Deception for Magicians" to "BeLIEve Me, But Cut the Cards: Understanding and Creating Magical Experiences" because I realized that the art of presenting magic involves more than the psychology of deception. Of course, the magic must be deceptive, but the philosophy, theatrical artistry, presentation, and audience management of the magic also have to be very strong to create magical experiences. As actor/magician Max Howard says, "It's not the tricks, it is everything else." I also saw that the changes matched my own life's interest and passions. From my teens and into adulthood my passions have been magic, psychology, philosophy, theology, and the theater arts.

More recently the column title was changed to "Make Believe: Discovering and Creating Magical Experiences." I made this change for several reasons: (1) the spelling "BeLIEve" is too closely identified for magicians with the now closed Las Vegas show and TV series, "Criss Angel BeLIEve;" and (2) the new title more clearly expresses what I am trying to say in the columns. Magical experiences, like good theater, are artistic and playful expressions of adult make believe.

I'm indebted to Robert Neale and Larry Hass for introducing me to the notion that magic is a form of "imaginative make believe." Make belief is an alternative to the belief vs. unbelief dichotomy and lies between the two. Neale places make believe, imagination, symbols, creativeness, playing and the transcendent in the "illusionistic world." This world lies between the "autistic" and "realistic" worlds of human existence (see the Appendix for more information about Pruyser's Three Worlds perspective). The idea of make believe is also found in the theater, especially Constantin Stanislavski's concept of the "Magic If" or "As If" in which the actors imagine that they are in a set of fictional circumstances and respond accordingly. Another acting teacher, Sanford Meisner, echoes the same when he defines "acting is the ability to live truthfully under imaginary circumstances." So with apologies to Jean Eugene Robert-Houdin, let me suggest that "a magician is an actor playing (make believing) the part of a magician."

The Wizard's *Scroll* columns were brief stand-alone reflections intended to express in a breezy style, concerns of magicians in understanding, creating and performing magical experiences for their various audiences. Quotes and references came from my readings, lecture notes, and conversations with magicians and other artists. The original newsletter columns have been significantly edited and revised for this publication. I have chosen to retain my sign-off phase at the end of each chapter, "Remember to cut the cards." The columns I've chosen for this collection are organized into chapters around three general themes: (1) psychology and philosophy; (2) creativity and the performing arts; and (3) the gift of receiving and giving magic. I've also included my close-up and stand-up performances pieces of three wonderful classics in magic: Scotch and Soda, the Egg Bag, and the Gypsy Thread.

Part I: Psychology and Philosophy

D. Michael Smith

1

A Psychology of
Deception for Magicians

"There is one way to find out if a man is honest- ask him, if he says 'yes,' he is
a crook." (Groucho Marx)

"Out of the crooked timber of humanity no straight thing can ever be made."
(Immanuel Kant)

"The heart is deceitful above all things, and desperately wicked: who can know
it?" (Jeremiah 17:9)

All three of these "philosophers" are, in their own ways, saying the same thing:
deception is part of the human condition. Deception simply means "the use of
deceit or the fact of being deceived." As magicians we publicly "celebrate our
transparency." We announce our innocent intentions and benign presence to
our audiences. We admit we lie in order to enchant and amuse. As Jamy Ian
Swiss likes to say, we are "honest liars." No one gets hurt. We are ambivalent
about con artists and card cheats. We love the process and methodologies of
these netherworld activities and will use them to entertain our audiences.

Take a brief trip into the places in our culture where deception can be seen.
Games and sports: we don't like it when someone cheats in games or sports,
but notice our language. We talk about a "fake pass" or a "stolen base" or a
"bluff." Advertising, marketing, and public relations: don't we assume that
deception will be a part of these activities? Law, politics, and public office:
need I say more?

Business and economics: remember Enron and the 2008 economic collapse.
The military and law enforcement: we assume and demand a certain amount of

deception to catch or defeat the "bad guys" but also dislike corrupt officers, prosecutors who want to win whatever it takes, and dishonest reasons to go to war. Religion, education and the sciences: distorted research, plagiarism, distorted financial records, inflated attendance numbers, and the covering up illegal and immoral behavior.

By far the most common form of deception is self-deception and interpersonal relations deception. We deceive ourselves and sometimes deceive those we love. Researchers, who ask people of all ages to keep tabs of all their falsehoods they told in the course of a week, found that 10% of the lies are mere exaggerations rather than frank deceptions (which makes up about 60% of lies). Some are subtle lies of omission. Many lies are told to smooth over awkward situations and protect egos and relationships. We deceive in order to obtain vicarious gratification and to create a sense of superiority over others. Lies have to do with self-esteem (we are not happy with ourselves). But some deceptions can deeply damage relationships and destroy trust.

When it comes to morality, we have two positions we live between in our culture. One position says deception is a perversion that undermines trust in society. The other position is deception (especially self-deception) is neither inherently moral nor immoral. It is an inextricable part of relationships with others.

So, what does all this have to do with performing magic? I think it speaks to our ambivalence as both audience members and as magicians. We like to be deceived, and yet we fight being deceived. We don't want to create an adversarial relationship with our audience (unless that is our magic character). We like to deceive and we want to be liked by others so we may feel "guilty" about deceiving. John Booth, himself a clergyperson and magician, says, "I am convinced that the element of guilt subconsciously creeps into the psyche of many who perform magic. . . . I have always contended that I have never seen a really outstanding clergy-conjurer . . . the traits that produce an exceptional church leader, often militate against effectiveness with legerdemain." Are we aware of any of these internal dynamics as we perform? How can we deal with these experiences? One answer for me is to approach my magic as an actor (remember Jean Eugene Robert-Houdini's famous quote, "a magician is an actor playing the part of a magician").

Till next time, remember to cut the cards.

2

Phenomenology

Phenomenology is a particular twentieth-century school of philosophy. It literally means "as it basically appears to us." It does not seek to analyze or explain life but rather wants to focus on living experience and our perceptions of life. Phenomenology holds that direct awareness forms the basis of truth. In its simplest form it means that "perception is reality." As the main character, Gabriel (played by John Travolta), a covert agent in the heist movie *Swordfish,* in a reference to the vanishing an elephant by Houdini, says, "What the eyes see and the ears hear, the mind believes." Phenomenology is a very diverse school of philosophy that has influenced psychology, religion, and the arts.

Now, this is where it applies to us magicians. Whether we know it or not, we are phenomenologists. We play with people's perceptions. Bob Neale's definition of magic is helpful here: "the artful performance of impossible things." Eugene Burger has reminded us that a good magical effect is constructed to have our audiences' internal sense be "that's fair . . . that's fair . . . that's fair—NO Way!!" As magicians, through both physical and psychological misdirection, we have for centuries been testing and exploiting the limits of cognition and attention of people.

Recently, like many of you, I saw the movie, *Now You See Me.* The running tag line in the movie is "the closer you look, the less you see." I will not give away the plot here in case you haven't seen it. If you want to know the story line and the characters see Wikipedia's summary. Let me just say the movie is about one magic trick within another magic trick within another magic trick. After I saw the movie, I read several film critics' reviews. I was struck by the fact that they seemed to either really hate the movie or really like the movie. One reviewer Roger Moore says, "The razzle dazzles, but smoke never quite hides the mirrors in *Now You See Me*, a super-slick new magicians' heist that demonstrates, once again, how tough it is for magic to work as a movie subject.

A medium that is by definition, a trick has a very hard time making illusions real, realistic and anything anyone would be impressed with." Another reviewer, Mike Johnston, says, *"Now You See Me* has some great tricks and even though we discover how they are done, it doesn't take away from the enthusiasm of the film. As with magic, what you are watching isn't always where the trick is happening. The same is true for some critics, what you are reading isn't always what you should expect in the theatre." Perception is reality.

As I read the above movie reviews that reflect the "culture wars" between film critics and magic, I was reminded of a comment by Larry Hass, in his lecture notes, *Deep Mental Mysteries*. In an essay, "Mentalism and Magic: An Essay on the Difference and Why It Matters," he talks about the "culture war" between magicians and mentalists. I think this essay is worth the cost of the notes (but there are some really good effects as well). He says, "For magicians and mentalists to criticize each other because the other group isn't creating the effects they like to create is like magicians criticizing clowns, actors whacking on musicians, dancers making fun of actors, musicians disparaging the jugglers, and all of them teaming up on the puppeteers. Common though this sniping may be among performing artists (and it is), much of it is narcissistic noise and misunderstanding based on fundamentally different paradigms of entertainment" (p. 28). Perception is reality.

Till next time, remember to cut the cards.

3

Meanings of 13

The month I wrote this marked the beginning of my 13th year (2013) with the Dallas Magic Clubs. I am lucky to have been included in this talented group of people committed to the art of magic. So, I thought I would focus on the number 13, especially as it relates to magic and magicians. It also has special meanings in mathematics, world religions, the occult, and the ideas of luck and fate. It is also embedded in our country's history (13 original colonies, 13 stripes on the flag).

Let me start with how the number 13 is especially important to the Dallas Magic Clubs. Remember, in addition to being Ring 174 of the International Brotherhood of Magicians, we are Assembly 13 of the Society of American Magicians. The Dallas Magic Club was originally organized in 1922, and then became the Dallas Magic Circle in 1924. We were scheduled to be Assembly 9 in the Society of American Magicians, but Dallas member Harry McDaniel held up the application until the number 13 became the next available Assembly number and then applied, saying that 13 is "not at all an unlucky number for us." Harry Houdini was performing at the State Fair of Texas in Dallas that year, and so, at the Adolphus Hotel on October 4, 1924, he installed the Dallas Magic Clubs Assembly as number 13. There were a total of fifteen members at the time. In 1964 we were installed as International Brotherhood of Magicians Willard the Wizard 174.

Both fear and luck are a part of the legacy of the number 13. The irrational fear of the number 13 is called "triskaidekaphobia," first used in 1910 in *Abnormal Psychology*. That fear is rooted in ancient history. There are 12.41 lunar cycles in a solar year. A year that contains 13 full moons instead of 12 posed problems for calendar makers in that it upset the regular arrangement of religious festivals. This was seen as unlucky by different cultures. The solar calendar won over the lunar calendar, and 13 became seen as a "curse." In our culture we see that "fear" being present when a hotel does not have a 13th floor. It is considered unlucky to have 13 guests at one table. Some sports figures avoid the number on their jerseys, while some actively seek to use the number. This fear has also been promoted by the slasher movie series, Friday the 13th. Our movies on witchcraft and the occult remind us that there are 13 full moons in a year, that there are 13 witches in a coven. Lucky 13 is seen in the "baker's dozen" or 12 + 1 cookies, etc. America's Apollo 13 space mission of 1970, featured in the 1995 Ron Howard movie, is referred to as the "successful failure."

In terms of magical presentations some of the above ideas could be used in your scripts especially around Halloween. Tony Corinda has *13 Steps to Mentalism* (1958). You might also check out Jim Steinmeyer's "Bermuda Triangle" in his *Impuzzibilities*. The 13th card in the Tarot Deck is the Death card. In our current decks the 13th card is the King. There are 13 cards in a suit. If you check YouTube you will find several 13 card tricks that you might find interesting and useful.

Till next time, remember to cut the cards.

4

Houdini's Box

In 2002, when I stopped by the H & R Magic Books display at a magic convention, Richard Hatch said that he had a book that he thought I would be interested in reading. Always valuing Richard's reading advice, I bought it, read it later, and then wrote a review of it for a professional counseling journal in 2003.* The title of the book is *Houdini's Box: The Art of Escape* by Adam Phillips, a British psychoanalyst whose therapeutic and literary style is very philosophical.

Phillips's thesis is that all of us are trying to escape from something, escape to somewhere else, or trying to "get away" with something. Phillips explores five very different escape artists. There is (1) Harry Houdini, famous magician and escape artist; (2) a little girl who plays an elaborate version of hide-and-seek in play therapy; (3) the Greek "ecstasy of flight" escape myth of Daedalus and Icarus; (4) a middle-aged academic patient who has become serially entranced with flight from women; and finally, (5) the nineteenth century poet Emily Dickinson, who spent the last twenty years of her life in self-imposed solitary confinement, but who used language as a liberator.

Phillips draws from one of the best Houdini biographies in his choice of Kenneth Silverman's *HOUDINI!!!: The Career of Ehrich Weiss* (1996). Every other chapter of his book focuses on the life and career of Houdini. Between these chapters are chapters that focus on the four other "escape artists." The title refers to one of Houdini's most famous illusions, "Metamorphosis." This illusion, first presented in 1895, is still performed today by a number of magicians. I still remember the first time I saw the Pendragons perform their version live at the Magic Castle in the 1980s. In 2001, *MAGIC Magazine* chose "Metamorphosis" as the best illusion of the twentieth century.

Phillips avoids (escapes?) psychoanalytic orthodoxy and makes the point that our sense of self is often shaped and defined by what endangers us. What we are trying to escape is, as Hungarian psychoanalyst Sandor Ferenczi suggests, shrouded in "mystery." Phillips says the Adam and Eve story of the Bible is "a great escape story, the story of a failed breakout. . . . The biblical story dramatizes, whatever else it does, the link in our minds between curiosity and release, and how our ideas of freedom depend upon our finding out what we fear."

Here are some questions about escape for us: When we perform, what are we trying to escape from? Escape to? Get away with? What about curiosity, release, fears? And what are our audiences trying to escape from, to, or get away with when they come to a magical performance? Jeff McBride says that there are two kinds of audiences: (1) some audiences are there to forget (fun and escape from); and (2) some audiences are there to remember (think, feel and escape to somewhere else). It is important to know what our audiences are expecting when we perform. Example: I don't perform a meaning-filled Robert Neale piece at a party, where people are drinking, engaged in small talk, and wanting to forget their cares, etc. If I do a magic trick in children's church on Sunday morning, I do something that will help people remember, think, and feel something deeply. What do you think?

Till next time, remember to cut the cards.

*American Journal of Pastoral Counseling, Vol. 6, #3, 2003, pp. 83-85

5

What Audiences
Really Think About Magic?

What I intend to do in this chapter is to summarize for you the results of a major study done on what audiences think about performance magic and magicians. This is drawn from *MAGIC Magazine*, Sept., 2016, pp. 46-55. This issue is the last issue published and came to only subscribers; therefore, many have not seen this report.

This comprehensive study was a partnership between magician Joshua Jay and Dr. Lisa Grimm and her research team in the Department of Psychology at The College of New Jersey. The study, "Magic by the Numbers," designed by Jay, Grimm, her team, and a number of others, involved 526 participants; 482 from the US and 44 from Europe, Latin American, and Asia. The ages ranged from 18 to 80 years; the average age of people tested is 30.8. The report uses both *qualitative data* (information not in numerical form, i.e. interviews, observations, etc.) and *quantitative data* (information in numerical form which can be put in categories, rankings, tables, etc.) on the topics of magic, magicians, and deception. Results show that a person's gender, age, and religious background affect how much they like magic and what kind of magic they like the best. In other words, before we do the first trick, our audiences bring their own "baggage" to our magic shows.

First surprising result: Magicians, as a group love card tricks. But, card magic is the least memorable of all types of magic to all audiences regardless of age, gender, and nationality. Audiences may remember that the magician did cards tricks but could not remember the effects. Only twenty-seven percent of participants could describe any card trick with any specificity. The most common response was to report "tricks with cards." Audiences remember effects that are easy to describe and understand. This a major challenge due to the fact that as a group, magicians love card tricks. The good news is that most people's recall of card tricks improved markedly when another prop or element was involved. Examples of this would be Cards to Pocket, Card in Lemon, Card on Ceiling, Signed Card to wherever, Shawn Farquhar's "Shape of My Heart" (with Sting's song), and René Lavand's elegant card artistry done with one hand to classical music. In magic we refer to these kinds of card tricks as tricks with "cards as objects." On a very personal note, I dislike many card tricks I see because they do not have much theatrical (story) value to me. This is one of the reasons why audiences can't easily recall card effects. When asked to name their "favorite magic trick," twenty percent of the respondents did mention card magic, despite being unable to describe it. This leaves us with the unanswered, but important, question, "If they enjoy what you do, does it matter if they remember specifics?" This is a question that needs further research.

What do people enjoy about magic? Seventeen percent just want to be "amazed," and fourteen percent like the mystery of magic best. Twelve percent like not knowing how the effects were done and ten percent like trying to figure out how the effects are done. Six percent of the respondents said they enjoyed the showmanship of the presentations. The "skill" of the magician was cited by 6% as their favorite. *Surprise!!!* Twenty-five percent like the element of surprise best. These people gravitated more strongly toward surprise, or as many said, "Not knowing what will happen next." So we have a paradox. Audiences expect to be surprised!!! It's like going on a roller coaster ride or to a scary movie where we expect to be scared! Playwright William Goldman captured the paradox when he wrote, "You must surprise an audience in an expected way."

The Bad News. What people dislike about magic shows is equally unexpected and almost unanimous. *People dislike when magicians do the same tricks.* Thirty-four percent (the most popular response) were concerned about the repetitive nature of a magician's material. These two results (people like surprise best and they dislike repetition most) challenges the sacred tenet of magic: "Do the classics." "The classics are classics for a reason," and "you can't go wrong with the classics." The main point here is to remember that the data suggests what a majority feels about various issues in magic, not how we think they should feel. The data suggests we should perform material unknown to our audiences, or find ways to frame classic effects in a surprising new way. *"Be original"* is the point and for the first time we have empirical data to back this statement up. The challenge for me is to take the classics in my act and present them in a unique way that includes a surprise ending.

Over all, how much do people like magic? When asked to rank their interest in a range of entertainment "seeing magic live" came in fourth (59%), behind seeing a film (81%), going to a concert (70%), and seeing a comedian (65%). Seeing a live magician was ahead of going to a party (54%), attending a play (45%) and watching a magician on television (31%). What did the respondents dislike about magic and magicians?: Thirty-four percent said, "performing old tricks;" twenty-four percent said "arrogant or cheesy performance style;" sixteen percent said "knowing how a trick is done;" fourteen percent said "not knowing how the trick is done;" six percent said "magic is boring;" and six percent "did not respond."

To summarize: (1) Card magic is the *least memorable* of all types of magic by magicians *except* when another prop, element, or well written script was included in the presentation. There seems to be a "weird" but important distinction for people between "card tricks" and "tricks with cards." (2) Audiences also do not like magicians doing the same tricks (Classics of Magic). They expect to be surprised and are disappointed when they see the same tricks presented in the same way performed by different performers without a surprise ending.

The full report (I encourage you to carefully read the complete study) has a lot more data that is very important and useful. You can see online Joshua Jay being interviewed by Jonathan Levit about the study that was recorded at the 2018 Magic Live conference. I wanted to focus on the above two items because they are two of our "golden calves" or idols- we love card tricks and we love doing the classics. Research on deception in our culture shows that self-deception is the most common form of deception we practice in our culture. There are many reasons, consciously and unconsciously, for self-deception.

Yes, it is true that Hofzinser once said that "card effects are the poetry of conjuring." But not all card tricks are poetry. Some strike me as bawdy limericks or worse. If you love and do card magic please read these two excellent chapters on this subject: "Are Card Tricks Card Magic?" in *Magic and Meaning* by Eugene Burger and Robert Neale and "How to Create Entertaining Card Magic" in *Inspirations: Performing Magic with Excellence* by Lawrence Hass. And yes, "the classics are classics for a reason." They are usually simple in their plot and easy to follow. But when we perform them can we make them our own with well written scripts and bring surprise to the endings to the effects.

To those magicians who criticize and reject the findings of the study Jay says, "Anyone who entirely rejects feedback from their audience is missing an amazing opportunity. Knowing *what your audiences think about magic* is important. Understanding *how your audience thinks about magic* is invaluable to anyone wishing to improve. . . . They (the study results) are tools, and the best magicians use every tool available to them."

Let me end with two very important results from this study. Of the 526 people (mostly from the USA and with an average age 30.8 years) who participated in the study, Twenty-eight percent have never seen a magician live, and only twenty-three percent have seen a magician within the last year. The next time you look out into your audience when you perform your close-up, parlor, or stage show, remember you may be the first magician that twenty-eight percent have ever seen or that over seventy-five percent have seen this year. We owe our audiences the best show we can.

Till next time, remember to cut the cards.

6

Self-Deception

"Yes, I have tricks in my pocket; I have things up my sleeve.
But I am the opposite of a stage magician. He gives you illusion that has the
appearance of truth. I give you truth in the pleasant disguise of illusion."

These words are from the opening soliloquy by Tom, in Tennessee William's memory play, *The Glass Menagerie*. Williams is intensely concerned with the conflict between imagination (illusion) and reality as seen in in his characters. He emphasizes the false relationships and lack of communication of his characters who engage in self-deception.

Self-deception is the most common form of deception in our lives. We do it for many reasons, consciously and unconsciously. What I want to explore here are the ways we magicians sometimes deceive ourselves as we prepare, practice, and rehearse our magic. The following are some of the ways I've experienced us practicing self-deception in our magic presentations.

- **Method that looks "odd" to lay people.** Examples of this are the way we sometimes handle playing cards. The Flushtration Count, Peek Control, Double Lift, the Elmsley Count, etc. are not the way most people handle cards. Larry Hass says that instead of "'settling for what we can get away with,' we need to aim for 'what will deceive the most vigilant members of the audience.'" My goal, which is not always reached, is to create the experience in the most observant lay person that follows Eugene Burgers' observation, "That's fair . . . that's fair . . . and that's fair . . . and that was fair. Whoa!! No way!"
- **Information overload and our search for the perfect magic effect**. While we need to continue to study and be open to new

ideas, we deceive ourselves when we buy this trick, book, DVD, etc. thinking it is the Holy Grail. We deceive ourselves when we don't settle in and do the hard work of practicing, scripting, and rehearsing, for the magic we have that is at our skill level.

- **Affective vs. analytical.** Most lay people want an affective experience when they see a magic show. They want to be emotionally moved in some way. Magicians usually engage in a more analytical process of understanding magic. This is why some magicians do not like to perform for other magicians. The responses are different. Several years ago at a Texas Association of Magicians convention I was sitting next to a well-known Texas member and stage technician who is now deceased. At the time I wanted to choke him! Throughout the stage show he was making critical remarks to his wife about the illusions, lighting, sound, music, blocking, etc. of the stage performers. He was engaged in a verbal critical analytical process, but this was intruding on my affective process (When I see an illusion show I am not, at that time, trying to analyze it. I just want to enjoy it and feel like an eleven year old boy again!)

- **Entertainment equals comedy.** Have you ever noticed that most magic is presented in a comical or humorous framework? I think this is why a lot of adults don't take magic seriously as an art form. Are all the movies and plays you see, concerts you attend, visual art exhibits you see presented as comedy or humor? Yes, some of the movies and dramas I see are comedies, some of the music I listen to is funny, and I love the comics. But I want these other art forms to move me emotionally in many other ways (Even the "comics" of my youth evolved to the graphic novels of today). All of these artistic expressions of our many different emotions can be entertaining. Of course, we have to be very aware of the audience expectations, venues, our personality, character, etc. in presenting our magic. But can we present some of our magic that can evoke other emotions? I think so. Think about it.

Till next time, remember to cut the cards.

7

Neuroscience and
Magic in the Classroom

"The most beautiful thing we can experience is the mysterious. It is the source
of all true art and science."
Albert Einstein

Magicians have been testing and exploiting the limits of cognition and
attention for hundreds of years. Psychologists and neuroscientists are
beginning to catch up by studying the ways magicians exploit mental lapses.
Leading the way has been Stephen Macknik, Ph.D. and Susanna Martinez-
Conde, Ph.D. in their *Scientific American* journal articles and their book,
*Sleights of Mind: What the Neuroscience of Magic Reveals About Our
Everyday Deceptions*, 2010. Recently, British psychologist Gustav Kuhn, in
his book, Experiencing *the Impossible: The Science of Magic*, 2019, has further
explored the science behind the magic. Years ago Houdini said, "What the
eyes see and ears hear, the mind believes."

For the last two years, Geoff Grimes and I have been presenting a magic
lecture each semester in all four of the introduction to psychology classes at
Mountain View College, in Dallas, Texas. We teach the section on the senses
and perception using magic to illustrate the points. **Sensations** (five senses) are
the process of taking in information from the environment. **Perception** is how
we recognize, interpret, and organize our sensations. Geoff and I demonstrate
the power of magical entertainment and misdirection to distort our senses and
confuse our conventional definitions and perceptions of reality. We use
examples of Impressionistic and Expressionistic art, optical illusions, humor,
and magical effects to demonstrate the psycho-neurological processes of
misdirection, change blindness, in-attentional blindness, choice blindness, and
illusory correlation. We demonstrate how our visual, auditory, and tactile
senses can be easily deceived.

Some of the "magical" effects that we use in our presentation are art prints of Claude Monet and Edvard Munch, and M. C. Escher; the Old Lady/Young Lady optical illusion; and Randi Rains' wonderful "Hare and Bird Superposition" that combines the Hippy-Hoppy Rabbits effect with a twist of the optical illusion of the rabbit and bird. We also do a sponge ball routine that includes a squeaker that fools the eyes and the ears; an Omni Deck card effect that fools the eyes and touch; and the "Princess Card Trick" with jumbo cards that demonstrates in-attentional blindness. For some fun and history we usually perform two classics of magic- the cups and balls and the egg bag. Our presentation always includes a YouTube video clip from *Scientific American* journal, "Neuroscience Meets Magic," that features Macknik and Martinez-Conde as well as the "Gentleman Thief," Apollo Robbins, a magician and pickpocket. We end the presentation with an handout and two warnings: (1) beware of con artists on the Internet and phone who appeal to our feelings of greed, fear, and compassion; and (2) the popular "myth of multitasking," especially believed by our plugged-in electronic culture.

So, what have we learned ourselves in these classes? Many young adults have not ever seen live magic before. Some have seen magic on TV or on social media but most have not seen a live magic show. We have learned that the students and all the psychology teachers like that we have taken "heavy" psychological and neuroscience concepts and presented them in an entertaining and understandable way. The school administration has also heard of our work. We were selected to do a day-long series of class presentations to local high school students who were on campus to experience a college class-room experience. What was the students' feedback? "Magic Rocks!"

Till next time, remember to cut the cards.

8

Bob Neale's "Magic & Meaning": An Index of Themes

"This is the best general theory of magic we have yet in any literature."
Lawrence Hass

One of magic's most profound and albeit disturbing philosophers, writers, and creators is Robert E. Neale. Bob retired early as a Psychology of Religion professor in order to write and a create origami and creative magic effects. Bob Neale invites the magic community to examine more deeply the foundations of our performance art. Yet, as challenging as he is, Bob's genius can inspire each of us to become better in our theatrical artistry, more thoughtful about our relationships with our audiences, and more appreciative of the services that magical entertainment continues to play in human communities.

It is difficult to penetrate the indefatigable mind of Bob Neale. To assist in the effort and with Bob's blessing and in consultation with Lawrence Hass, Dean of McBride's Magic & Mystery School, Geoff Grimes and I began in 2016 to identify and index 13 essential themes that emerge in his 18 books and 1 DVD, ranging from *In Praise of Play* (1969) *to Breaking Our Magic Wands* (2017).

As a philosopher Bob is a phenomenologist, one who studies human experiences. To study magical experiences, he draws upon the insights from psychology, philosophy, theology, cultural anthropology, mythology, literature, and sociology. In 2014 Bob was the recipient of a Special Fellowship from the Academy of Magical Arts in Hollywood, California (the Magic Castle).

Geoff and I presented the completed index to Bob and the magic community on October 24, 2018, at the McBride Magic & Mystery School "Magic and Meaning Conference" in Las Vegas, Nevada.

Geoff Grimes, Bob Neale, and Mike

<u>The Thirteen Essential Themes</u>
Play
The Trickster Spirit
Paul Pruyser's Three Worlds Perspective
The Imagination
Wonder
Illusions
Magic
The Magician(s)
Off-Stage/On-stage Magic
Performance
Psychological Classification of Magic
The Ethical heart of Spiritual Illusions: "The Four Falls"
Life and Death and . . .

Just a word about what we are not attempting to do in this index and why. We are not attempting to introduce Bob's works. This has been done in his three volumes, *The Trilogy of Magic*. Neither are we attempting to interpret/criticize Bob's thoughts. Finally, we haven't extended our analysis into the hundreds of performance pieces, published in his many books, lecture notes, articles, and so on. What we have done is introduce Bob, as a person, provide a selected bibliography, and list the thirteen themes (and sub-themes) we believe best capture Neale's "general theory of magic."

Remember that an index is a section of a book or article that provides a list of subjects in printed works with the page number where each subject can be found. This is helpful if you want to focus in on one or more of the themes (or sub-themes).

To see the full twenty-two page index go online to the site provided by Theory and Art of Magic Press:

http://www.theoryandartofmagic.com/samples/download/the-robert-e-neale-index.

Till next time, remember to cut the cards.

9

Positive Illusions

"Where there's a will, a way will be created."
George Parker

We magicians are in the illusion business. Illusions are our stock and trade. We love illusions (sleight of hand, stage, optical, mental/psychological, and so on). But when the "muggles in our mist" use the word illusion in everyday speech, they usually mean one of the following three meanings:

1. "a thing is or is likely wrongly perceived or interpreted by the senses"
2. "a deceptive appearance or impression"
3. "a false idea or belief"

Some of the synonyms used for illusion include mirage, hallucination, fantasy, vision, sham, pretense, delusion, deception, misconception, etc. Often, in common usage, illusion has a negative connotation. So, except when used for entertainment purposes, illusions are usually seen as something negative.

In the mid-1970s psychologists began to study what came to be known as "positive illusions." Basically, positive illusion studies have shown that human thoughts are positively biased compared to what is realistically possible. In 1988 Taylor and Brown theorized that positive illusions are necessary for good mental health. In her 1989 book, *Positive Illusions: Creative Self-Deception and the Healthy Mind*, author Shelley E. Taylor says, "My task in this volume is to persuade the reader that normal human thought and perception is marked not by accuracy but by positive self-enhancing illusions about the self, the world, and the future. . . . They appear actually to be adaptive, promoting rather than undermining good mental health" (p.7). She further says, "Illusions fall into three general categories: self-enhancement, or the perception of one's self, one's past behavior, and one's enduring attributes as more positive than is actually the case" (p. 6). Taylor's view of illusions is very different from past psychological approaches that claim positive self-enhancement is maladaptive. By 2001 Robins and Beer were arguing that it is time to acknowledge the existence of positive illusions as a fact and start looking at the findings in context.

What does all this say to us magicians? Well, for me, it says that what magic philosophers, Robert Neale and Larry Hass call "Life Magic" is right on target. (Thanks Larry for pointing me to Shelley's above quoted book.) In his book, *Life Magic: Ideas and Mysteries*, 2018, Larry credits Robert Neale for the concept of Life Magic (See *An Essay on Magic*, pp. 50-54, 2015). Life Magic refers to our everyday magical performances, "the subtle spells rituals, illusions, and incantations that play an indispensable part in a happy, healthy, and flourishing life" (*Life Magic*, p. 29). They are usually those every day, commonplace beliefs, words, and acts that have gone unnoticed for so long that they have become almost invisible.

Examples of these "unknown thoughts" include positive self-talk; believing we control our environment; thinking that tomorrow will be similar to today; and all the beliefs, words, objects, and actions that calm and soothe us. But the positive illusion that is most related to performance magic is theatrical and movie performances. This is Life Magic at its best. When viewing movies and dramas, we are deeply involved in "make believe." We get drawn into the scenes, characters, and actions. Make believe is not a delusion, superstition, or mere deception. It is a form of play. In fact, we refer to a drama as a play. "Make believe" play gives health, pleasure, love, hope and calmness. In other words, these experiences can be life enhancing.

And so, may our "make believe" magic performances bring life-enhancing experiences to our audiences.

Till next time, remember to cut the cards.

Performance Piece 1

A Fantasy Vacation

Effect: You (the magician) are performing for a family at a restaurant. You ask if the family would like to take a fantasy family vacation. With the answer "yes," you explain that you will serve as their travel agent. As you are speaking, you take a small coin pursue from your pocket and remove and display in your hand three coins- a half dollar, a Mexican 20 Centavos coin, and a Canadian two dollar (toonie) coin. You then place the coins in the hand of one of the adults, asking them to tightly hold them. You now explain that you want the family to plan a fantasy vacation from the United States to either Mexico or Canada. You explain that they need to decide together which country they will visit. The family members discuss and decide whether to go to Canada or Mexico. When the family decides the destination, the adult who is holding the three coins opens their hand and discovers that the Mexican coin has vanished, leaving the half and the toonie. The Mexican coin is discovered to have returned to the purse which has been lying in full sight on the table.

Method: This is done with a commercial Scotch and Soda gimmick along with a Canadian toonie (instead of a quarter) as well as a legitimate Mexican 20 Centavos coin. All are placed in a small coin purse. When you remove the three coins from the purse, remove only the half dollar shell, the toonie, and the 20 Centavos insert upmost in your hand. Leave the legitimate 20 Centavos coin in the purse which you close and lay on the table. When you place the three coins in the spectator's hand, be sure the half dollar shell is above the 20 Centavos insert and the toonie under them. When they close their hand, the half shell will lock over the Centavos, leaving only two coins, the half and the toonie, in the spectator's fist.

Ending: The ending of the effect will vary depending on what country the family chooses for their vacation. (1) If they choose **Canada,** have the spectator open her hand, and you say, "You now can go from the United States to Canada for your fantasy vacation." Then have the spectator open the purse and say, "You now have the centavo saved for a later trip to Mexico." (2) If they choose **Mexico,** then have them open the purse and say, "Your Mexican coin is packed away in your luggage ready for your fantasy vacation to Mexico. You are left with the Canadian coin to save for a later vacation."

D. Michael Smith

Part II: Creativity and the Performing Arts

10

The Magician's Choice

One of the most useful psychological tools that a good magician or mentalist has in their verbal "toolbox" is the ability to know how and when to use the "Magician's Choice." Known also as "equivoque," the Magician's Choice is the ability to interpret a spectator's apparently free choice(s) in such a way as to execute a force that the entertainer wants. Phil Goldstein says, "In essence equivoque is the process of psychological forcing combined with double entendre." When done well it is a work of art. It truly is "sleight of mind" at its best. When done poorly, it is usually obvious to the spectator.

I was first introduced to equivoque in 1976 in an eight-page mimeographed booklet entitled *Verbal Control: A Treatise on the Underexplored Art of Equivoque; Technique and Applications* by Phil Goldstein (Max Maven). You can Google it on the Internet. Max also produced an excellent DVD on equivoque in 2010 entitled, *Multiplicity.* In my opinion one of the very best packet mental card tricks is Maven's "B'wave." I use it for close-up with regular-size cards and have a jumbo stage-size version. Read and follow his instructions carefully, and you will experience a good example of equivoque. Another excellent resource is chapters 8-11 of *The Mental Mysteries of Hector Chadwick*, revised edition, 2008.

An interesting novel was published with the title, *Magician's Choice*, 2013. It is the second novel written by Todd Gipstein who is a writer, photographer, and producer. He says that he has loved magic since his mother gave him his first magic set when he was ten years old. He admits he has a lifelong addiction to buying and collecting magic apparatus and posters as well as performing close-up magic. Gipstein's knowledge of magic and magic history, especially in the Thirties and Forties, is very evident in this novel.

Magician's Choice is the story of a magician, Guy Borden, who first was bitten by the magic bug when his mother took him to see Harry Blackstone, Sr. for his tenth birthday. He had a chance to meet the great Blackstone who taught him the retention vanish with a silver dollar and also mailed him a magic kit. He continued his love of magic through high school and into the military during WWII. After being wounded in combat and being released from the military, he joined a traveling carnival as a magician. He eventually made his way to New York and came to meet and know a number of well-known magicians including Dai Vernon, Harry Blackstone, Lou Tannen, Charlie Miller, Faucett Ross, Ross Bertram, Al Baker, Francis Carlyle, and Theo Bamberg. He eventually becomes an outstanding performer, marries a woman he met when travelling with the carnival, and confronts another magician who had betrayed him.

In the final chapters, we see that he (and we, the readers) have experienced something of the magician's choice as he makes career and personal choices and learns some important lessons about life and death, friendship, love, betrayal, revenge, and forgiveness. Guy (and we, the readers) are challenged to question the place that fate, fortune, and destiny plays in our lives. As Gay Blackstone says in the Foreword to the novel, "There are lots of twists and turns in this story. Many mysteries within the world of mysteries. . . . The story itself is like a magic trick, an illusion grounded in reality that yet partakes of dreams."

Till next time, remember to cut the cards.

11

WOW!!!

"People say that what we're all seeking is a meaning of life. I don't think that's what we're really seeking. I think that what we're seeking is an experience of being alive . . . so that we actually feel the rapture of being alive."
Joseph Campbell

Larry Hass, in his essay, "Ways of Wonder," reminds us that Plato got it wrong. Plato (427-347 BC) contended in his *Republic* that lovers of the arts are bewitched by the deceptions of the senses, saying that they are the "victims of magic." He is arguing that philosophy is about truth and magic is about the false. But, to his credit, he then says something remarkable in his dialogue "Theaetetus," when he quotes Socrates who said, "The sense of wonder is the mark of the philosopher."

This month I want us to consider wonder, awe, astonishment, marvel, curiosity, and surprise. In other words, the feeling of WOW!!! I think this is important to us magicians for three reasons: (1) most of us were first drawn to this art form because we experienced those feelings ourselves; (2) we want to continue to experience those feelings; and (3) those feelings are what we want to help create in those who see our magic. In other words we want to "feel the rapture of being alive."

René Descartes (1596-1650), French philosopher and mathematician and considered the father of modern philosophy, in his *The Passions of the Soul*, argues that wonder is "the first of all passions." Without wonder to inspire the other passions (love, hatred, desire, joy, and sadness), we don't feel them as passions and our lives are diminished. Two excellent resources on wonder is "Ways of Wonder: Philosophy and the Art of Magic," in *Transformations: Creating Magic Out of Tricks*, Larry Hass, 2007, pp. 151-161 and Robert

Neale's book, *The Sense of Wonder*, 2014.

Our word "wow" is from a sixteenth-century Scottish word. Robert Burns used it in 1791 in his poem, "Tam o' Shanter": "An', wow! Tam saw an unco sight!" ("Unco" means strange and unfamiliar). The dictionary has three meanings for wow: (1) an indication of excitement or surprise; (2) an expression of amazement or awe; and (3) used sarcastically to express disapproval of something (as in "Wow! I can't believe you would do such a thing).

What I want to experience and what I want my audiences to experience are found in the first two definitions. I don't want to experience or my audience to experience the third definition. So the task is great. What can we do to so deepen our magical methods and presentations to make this response more likely? I close with these words from Anne Lamott from her 2012 remarkable little book, *Help, Thanks, Wow: the Three Essential Prayers*:

"When we are stunned to the place beyond words, we're finally starting to get somewhere. It is so much more comfortable to think that we know what it all means, what to expect and how it all hangs together. When we are stunned to the place beyond words, when an aspect of life takes us away from being able to chip away at something until it's down to a manageable size and then to file it nicely away, when all we can say in response is 'Wow,' that's a prayer" (p.73).

Till next time, remember to cut the cards.

12

Meisner and Magic

"Acting is the ability to live truthfully under imaginary circumstances."
Sanford Meisner

One of the things I like about coming from a psychology and philosophy background is that it allows me to "dabble" in a lot of different areas. Just use the phase, "the psychology of ___" or "the philosophy of___" and I can explore many different fields. My personal experience with acting was long ago in high school and the first two years of college when I was a drama major. But I have long felt that the skills of the actor are important for magicians to study.

In 1994 I attended a day-long workshop sponsored by the Baylor University Drama Department led by Cash Baxter on the "Meisner Method" of acting. Baxter split his time between New York City where he was a Broadway director, Southern California, and Houston where he was Distinguished Professor of Theater at the University of Houston. Baxter was a student of Sanford Meisner (1905-1997). Meisner's approach to acting focuses, not on thinking or feeling, but on *doing*. In contrast to the other two giants of American drama teachers, Lee Strasberg and Stella Adler, Meisner's approach has been called the "behavioral strand" of the Stanislavski systems. His exercises help us to live truthfully (behave) in the imaginary circumstances of being a magician to what we get from our audiences, assistants, or routines. In the workshop we did two of his exercises, the "pinch and ouch" and the "word repetition game." He said that the source of fear for actors (and magicians?) is not knowing our lines and watching ourselves. I went away from this workshop convinced that Meisner had something to teach magicians about presentation.

In the years following this experience several other experiences reinforced my belief that Meisner had something to contribute to magic. First, David Mamet, Broadway director of Ricky Jay's three award winning Broadway magic shows and several of the movies that Ricky has starred in, was a student of Sanford Meisner. Mamet can be seen in the DVD, *"Deceptive Practice: the Mysteries and Mentors of Ricky Jay."* Mamet says, "The audience sees the illusion of a character upon the stage . . . the magician created an illusion in the mind of the audience. So does the actor . . . acting is living truthfully under the imaginary circumstances of the play." Second, Jay Sanky, in his 2003 book, *Beyond Secrets*, says, "To learn about acting, I urge you to read *Sanford Meisner on Acting*. It makes for a marvelous introduction." Also see *Sanford Meisner Master Class*, a two DVD set of eight hours of acting instruction.

Jonathan Levit, magician and actor, describes in his lecture note, *Musings*, acting as an experience of "living truthfully under imaginary circumstances." "One of my acting teachers was in a show, and at one point there were three scenes going at the same time on stage. And in one of the scenes there was a bagel, and the bagel accidentally got hurled into one of the other scenes. And the actors in that other scene just went about their business, as if there were no bagel. So the point is, don't ignore the bagel. . . . Don't ignore what happens to you on stage. . . . So being relaxed, being real, and not ignoring the bagel— not ignoring what is happening around you. And don't ignore what happens in the audience." This is "truthful living" under the imaginary circumstances of the performance.

Till next time, remember to cut the cards.

13

Surrealism and Magic

"Magic, perhaps more than any other art form, has the ability to tear a hole in our maps of reality."
David Parr

Most of us as we mature in our practice of magic move away from the tubes and "tricky boxes" that had such a strong appeal to us as young magicians. We usually discover that more powerful magic is usually created with an everyday, recognizable object. Cards, money, rope, handkerchiefs, jewelry, cups, balls, etc. become the objects we work our magic. David Parr, a Chicago magician, calls this the "Wonder of the Ordinary."

What we do with these common objects is to set up situations where, as Eugene Burger explains, the audience members say, "That was fair—that was fair—and that was fair—and, yes, that was fair. Whoah!! No freaking way!" That is the magic moment. Another way of saying this is "That looks real, normal, etc. that looks real, normal, etc. and that looks real, normal, etc. Whoah!! No freaking way is that real, normal, etc.!" This is what David Parr means about "tearing a hole in our maps of reality." "Conjuring, like the art of M. C. Escher, can derive power from things that are 'recognizable to everyone.' Magic lies hidden just beneath the surface of the commonplace" (Parr, p. 50).

The above dynamic also occurs in Surrealistic art. This branch of modern art, which finds its sources in the unconscious and subconscious, makes us "look at everyday objects in delightfully new ways by surprising us with strange juxtapositions and bizarre distortions of reality, in much the same way magicians do" (Parr, pp. 47-48). Surrealism came out of the devastating carnage of World War I in Europe and is highly symbolic. Unlike the realistic, rational works that had come before, the works of these artists were getting their spectators to actively engage with them. "It was this engagement, this love of whimsy and the bizarre, which captured the interest of Jeff Sheridan" (*MAGIC Magazine*, Nov., 1998, p. 67).

Sheridan, a New York magician, rediscovered street magic in the 1960s and '70s (see *Street Magic* by Edward Claflin, 1977). Sheridan studied at the School of Visual Arts and in September, 1998 created a New York City art exhibit, "Jeff Sheridan: The Surrealist's Magician." The exhibit featured some magic objects (cards, fan, scissors, scotch tape, multiplying pipes, etc.). Like the Surrealist artists, Magritte, Dali, Ernst, Man Ray, and Escher, Sheridan challenged his audiences to "come to their own conclusions about life and death, while musing over his resting tricks. Along with magic, then, he turned to the Surrealistic technique of object-making to provoke onlookers into deeper thinking" (*Genii: The Conjuror's Magazine*, Nov., 1998, p. 68).

Till next time, remember to cut the cards.

14

Magicians and Actors
Part 1

"A magician is an actor playing the role of a magician."
Jean-Eugene Robert Houdin

"It's not the tricks, it is everything else."
Max Howard

"Anytime magic is performed . . ., it is the performance of theater. . . .
Whether you like it or not, whether you are interested in it or not, good theater
or bad, it will always be theater."
Tommy Wonder

Since my retirement I have been in a senior adult theater group at Theatre Arlington in Arlington, Texas. My past theater experience was in high school and in college as well some workshop experiences. My goal was not to become an actor so much as to become a "theatrically-skilled magician." Three magicians who have helped me through their writings and personal contact are Max Howard, Bob Fitch, and Lawrence Hass. The acting teachers whose writings have instructed me are Konstantin Stanislavsky, Sanford Meisner, and David Mamet. In the next two chapters I am presenting some of the notes I've prepared for a lecture/workshop I did with two delightful Dallas-Fort Worth theater actors, dancers and directors, Tracie Foster Stein and Maggie Younkin.

In this chapter I am highlighting the similarities between acting and magic. In the next chapter I will highlight some of the ways that acting and magic are different. My hope is that both magicians and actors will appreciate the contributions that each brings to the theatrical experience.

The following are some of the past and present magicians that I am aware of who had/have theatrical training: Orson Wells, Channing Pollock, Coe Norton, John Calvert, Ricky Jay, Jonathan Levit, Bob Fitch, Max Howard, Rob Zabrecky, Neal Patrick Harris, Steve Valentine, Tommy Wonder, Tom Mullica, John Tudor, Harry Anderson, and Larry Hass.

Similarities of Acting and Magic

1. Both the magician and the actor are "honest liars." When both perform they both are upfront that what you will see is not literally true even though truth is presented.

2. Both operate between belief and disbelief—"Make-belief."

3. Both ask the audience to suspend their disbelief, but in some different ways (more about these differences next time).

4. Both hide their technique in their presentations. A magician can "blow" a move and an actor can "over-act" or forget their lines. Good performances require that these things do not happen.

5. Both use the physical and psychological secrets that fool the mind - eyes, voice, hands, body, and feet (see *The Five Points of Magic* by Juan Tamariz).

6. Both operate on the belief that "what the eyes see and the ears hear, the mind believes." (Harry Houdini)

7. Both the magician and actor can greatly benefit from improvisation training, especially with dealing with unplanned events in a performance.

8. A one man/woman theatrical show is, in many ways, like a magician performing alone on the stage.

9. Both can benefit from the skills of the other: magicians can benefit from the theatrical skills of the actor and the actor can learn about the art of creating illusions on stage. A number of recent Broadway shows/musicals make use of magical consultants (i.e., Jim Steinmeyer, Paul Kieve, and Chris Fister).

As I end this chapter and to anticipate the next part, "Some Differences between Actors and Magicians" I want to close with this quote from actor and magician Max Howard:

"It is curious that actors and magicians approach their work in such different ways because both perform for live audiences in real time, both must be seen and heard in order to be understood, both must make emotional connections, causing tears and fears and laughter and both must create an environment in which the impossible happens. Actors do create magic. Magicians are telling a story" (*Theatre Technique for Magicians*, 1999, p.5).

Till next time, remember to cut the cards.

15

Magicians and Actors
Part 2

Some Differences between Magicians and Actors

"Actors do create magic. Magicians are telling a story."
Max Howard

In the last chapter I outlined some the ways that magicians and actors are similar. In this chapter I want to highlight some of the major differences between these performers.

1. Magicians are trick-driven. We usually start with a trick. Actors are story or script driven. Actors start with a play/show script.

2. Magicians usually have to do it all- magic, character development, script, costumes, music, directing, etc. Actors in the theater or in film/TV usually have others with these responsibilities.

3. Magicians often appear alone on stage while actors most often relate to other actors on stage.

4. The "fourth wall" is usually in place for actors; a magician usually breaks that wall and relates directly with the audience. Audience members are not invited on the stage with the actor but are often invited on to the stage with the magician.

5. "Character" is defined for the actor by the story/script and actors play many different roles. The magician usually plays one role and develops his/her character or "persona." Eberhard Riese reminds us there are only three basic roles/types of magicians possible: the Killer,

the Victim and the Witness.

    * The Killer causes the magical effect and is in control.

    * The Victim is taken by surprise by the magic (just like the audience), "suffers"   from it and is blown away by it.

    * The Witness reports the magical effect and coexists with it.

6.   The scripts of magicians evolve from their character/persona. Here are some current examples:

    * The Killer causes the magical effect and is in control.

    * Ricky Jay- arrogant, erudite historian

    * Penn- loud, brash skeptic

    * Teller- silent, puckish imp

    * Chris angel- rock star

    * David Copperfield-superstar

    * David Blaine- mysterious stranger

    * Mac King- country bumpkin

    * Doug Henning- flower child

    * Harry Anderson- loveable con man

7.   Audience Expectations- Both the actor and the magician require the audience to "suspend disbelief," but in different ways. Years ago my family and I saw *Peter Pan* at the Kennedy Center in Washington, D.C. In the show Peter and the children fly in the air. Everyone in the audience could see the wires on the body harnesses. But this reality did not distract from the story and the production. The audience "suspended disbelief," and went along with the story, and were not bothered by the wires. David Copperfield flies in his stage show. If we, the audience, see the wires on David the magic is over and gone.

Lawrence Hass says it this way, "Unlike traditional theater, magic theater requires visceral, felt experiences of impossibility ('No way!!!'). If you don't fool 'em, it ain't magic." It is very interesting that many recent stage shows and musicals have employed "magical consultants" to bring this added "fool 'em" to their productions.

To conclude I want to list some books and DVDs on magic and the theatrical arts that I have found to be very helpful:

* *Inspirations: Performing Magic with Excellence,* Lawrence Hass, 2015

* *Creating Theatrical Magic* (with DVD), Max Howard, 2014

* *Theatre Technique for Magicians*, Max Howard, 1999

* *Sharing My Secrets,* Bob Fitch, 2001

* *Ahead of the Game,* Jonathan Levit (2-DVD set), 2014

* *Scripting Magic,* Peter McCabe, 2007

* *The Show Doctor,* Jeff McBride, 2012

* *Foundations: the Art of Staging Magic,* Eberhard Riese, 2006

* *The Five Points of Magic,* Juan Tamariz, 2007

* *A Practical Handbook for the Actor,* Melissa Bruder and others, 1986

* *An Actor's Companion,* Seth Barrish, 2015

Till next time, remember to cut the cards.

16

Creating a Magical Effect and a Show

Recently I led a mini-workshop for the Fort Worth Magicians Club on the subject of "Creating a Magical Effect and a Show." Several members presented single pieces of magic to the group and then we used some of the material below to guide a discussion of the presentations. We focused especially on the three Samelson questions below.

Peter Samelson is a New York-based magician; author of *Theatrical Close-Up* and the 2016 *M-U-M* series, "Twelve Unholy Essays; "and creator of the magical effects, "The Phoenix" (burned and restored napkin) and "Heartstrings" (gypsy thread).

Samelson asks three questions (from *Genii: The Conjurors' Magazine*, Sept., 2014, p. 55) which can be summarized as "**Why, What**, and **Who**?"

WHY?

1. Why am I doing this?

2. Why should anyone want to watch this?

3. What is your reason for performing? Fooling is not a reason, just a technique. What does someone gain from watching me perform?

WHAT?

1. What is this piece about?

2. What would it look like if it were "real magic"?

3. Since magic is an imagistic art and communicates through its

symbolism, each piece must have an inherent meaning. What is it? If it is to work as magic, it must look like magic. What would that be?

WHO?

1. Who are you doing this for, who is your audience?

2. Who are you in this presentation; what is your character or persona?

Know yourself; know your work; and know your audience (age range, economic strata, education, and environment). Who are they? What do they want? And who is your character?

As we create an individual effect, we need to remember that most likely this effect is only one part of a set or a show. As Larry Hass, Dean of the McBride Magic & Mystery School and author of *Inspirations: Performing Magic with Excellence* reminds us in chapter twenty-one, "The fundamental unit of magic is the show, not a trick." Hass believes that a show needs a Beginning effect (needs to be *engaging*), Middle effects (needs to be *interesting*), and an Ending effect (needs to have a *punch—"POW" or "heart"*). The other factor to be considered as we create an effect and/or show is who your audience is. Hass adds that if your show is only one routine, then you need to select one that itself contains an engaging opening, interesting middle, and a punchy ending-the same dramatic curve.

To illustrate beginning, middle, and ending effects, I want to honor Eugene Burger, who died in 2017 and use some of his well-known magic effects that I like. Two of Eugene's opening effects were "The Pack That Cuts Itself," and "The Four Coin Opener." Three of his middle effects were "Thirteen for Dinner," "The Inquisition," and "Fading Coin." And, of course, his closing effect was almost always the "Cosmic Thread."

Till next time, remember to cut the cards.

17

To Do or Not to Do, That Is the Question

Maybe it is because I turned seventy-six this year, but recently I have been thinking a great deal about time, especially in terms of how much time I have left and what am I doing with the time I have now. These questions are true for all of us if we are honest. So, I was especially drawn to a specific chapter in George Parker's new book, *Performing Magic with Impact* (Theory and Art of Magic Press, 2018). George was the main presenter at the October, 2018 "Magic and Meaning Conference" in Las Vegas. George is an international speaker, storyteller, and stand-up magician. With a background in psychology, philosophy, health care, and organizational management, he has dedicated his life to exploring and inspiring the process of transformation in persons and organizations.

The chapter, "The Impact to Effort Ratio," discusses the relationship between the impact of our magic on the audience and the amount of effort (time, money, energy, love) we put in to create that impact. He calls this the "Impact-to-Effort-Ratio (IER). He talks about "high" and "low" impact and "high" and "low" effort. Some of the classics of magic such as the Torn and Restored Newspaper, Cardiographic, B'Wave, Card Warp, and the Invisible Deck have a "high impact" but rather "low effort" ratio. Some difficult sleight of hand effects have both high impact and high effort. A well-performed cups and balls routine is also a high impact and high effort effect. Unfortunately, much of the magic we see marketed is both low impact and low effort. Generally, we magicians seek the high impact and low effort magic effects.

Sometimes, we are drawn to effects that have a low impact and high effort. For the last four or five years I have worked off and on two card pieces that involve Shakespearean characters as the court cards. I have taken a lot of time thinking and talking to several different theatrical directors and magic consultants about different ways to present these to my audiences. While the effects are not that difficult to perform, the "wow" factor is low. Another difficulty is that, while I love Shakespeare's plays, most of my audiences are not that familiar or interested in Shakespearean plays. So, where would I present these effects? In truth, both of these card effects are really close-up pieces that I want to present in my stand-up act. This would require creating larger props and a costume to transport. As you can begin to see, this is high effort with low impact. So, while I love the possibility of playing Prospero (*The Tempest*), I'm letting this one go. What I plan to do with my time is to focus on mostly high-impact magic classics that fit my character with different scripts I write that can be presented to my two or three target audiences. So you, dear readers (and with an apology to Hamlet), have to decide for yourselves what "to do or not to do."

Till next time, remember to cut the cards.

18

Magic: The Art of Being Silly and Serious

"Philosophy is concerned with two matters: soluble questions that are trivial, and crucial questions that are insoluble."

"It is important to be serious about the silly and silly about the serious."

Now, before some of you stop reading, please know I will be relating these quotes to the practice of magic. The first is a quote is from Martin Gardner's *The Ways of a Philosophical Scrivener*. The second is from Robert E. Neale's *Magic Matters*. Both of these philosophers were/are magicians. The question for us is how do we each find the balance in our magical presentations between too light (trivial/silly) and too heavy (insoluble/serious)? It is also a question I ask myself frequently.

Before I retired as a therapist and educator I read professional journals that included a lot of behavioral research (serious). One of the questions I frequently asked myself is, "Are we measuring what is really valuable (serious?), or are we valuing what is only measurable (silly?)?" Measurable and valuable are not always the same. I think this question could be asked of a number of different endeavors: science, education, religion, business, the arts and entertainment. This brings me back to magic. For us, magic is a form of entertainment and artistic expression. One of the reasons magic is often not taken seriously by many as an art form is that it is seen as trivial/silly (minor entertainment for children). Even if we may try to present it as mentalism, bizarre "magick," or as Gospel magic, which deal with insoluble/serious themes, it is experienced by many as trivial or superficial.

For me the way that we as magicians can find the best balance between the silly and serious is the creative use of *humor, playfulness, and imagination.*

Ever since I first saw the Robin Williams movie, *Patch Adams*, some years ago, I've been interested in the healing power of humor. Consider the following quotes about the power of humor and laughter:

* "A cheerful heart is good medicine, but a downcast spirit dries up the bones." (Proverbs 17:22)

* "Against the assault of laughter nothing can stand." (Mark Twain)

* "Humor is emotional chaos remembered in tranquility." (James Thurber)

* "Anything worth taking seriously is worth making fun of." (Tom Lehrer)

* "Children laugh about 400 times a day; adults perhaps 15 times a day." (*APA Monitor*, March, 1999)

If you want to get "serious about humor," check out the Association for Applied and Therapeutic Humor (www.AATH.org). The first academic degree in "medical clowning" is available in Israel, and in the USA the Big Apple Circus has helped train and place "clown doctors" in more than eighteen facilities nationwide. Rob Divers, RN, known as "Magic Nurse Bob" is a Dallas area pediatric nurse who uses magic and clowning to care for children. Check out his book, *Magic Nurse—Bedside Artist* (2017). I am not naturally "funny," but I can be humorous. I try to use humor in my magical presentations (stand-up and close-up). I laughed a lot as a counselor, even though my "day job" dealt with many serious and, in some cases, insoluble issues. In my counseling practice I used humor, surprise, exaggeration, absurdity, wordplay, metaphorical mirth, tragic/comic twist, and confrontation/affirmation humor. We all can use our particular forms of humor in our magical presentations.

Till next time, remember to cut the cards.

19

The Wizard of Us

"Like all great stories, *The Wizard of Oz* provides a template that allows us to open ourselves to the hidden capacities we had forgotten we had; the creative potentials we didn't know how to use; and the deeper knowing . . . that is within every one of us. We are so much more than we thought we were."
Jean Houston

"Artists are driven by the tension between the desire to communicate and the desire to hide."
D. W. Winnicott

When I was five years old, I saw the movie, *The Wizard of Oz*. I was terrified of the Wicked Witch and her Flying Monkeys. As I got older, my fears eased, and the movie eventually became one of my favorites. Still later, I studied the book by L. Frank Baum and became intrigued with the symbolic meanings of the various characters in the story. If you haven't ever seen the movie, please stop now, and see it online, DVD, or on the TCM television station. Or better yet, read the book. I recommend *The Annotated Wizard of Oz* by Baum, with Notes by Michael Hearn, and Preface by Martin Gardner (2000). This story, what Joseph Campbell calls a "Hero's Journey," has become an American cultural myth that allows us, the audience, to enter a magical reality.

As a psychotherapist I sometimes used the characters from the Wizard of Oz as metaphors for some of the personal and relational problems that clients brought to therapy. Scarecrow went to Oz in search of a brain. Some clients needed to focus on their faulty thinking, especially about themselves, others, and the world. This is called Cognitive Therapy. Some clients, like Tin Man, needed to be more aware of their feelings, their heart. This is called Affective Therapy. Some clients came to find courage, like the Cowardly Lion, to behave in brave and healthy ways. This is called Behavioral Therapy. Like Dorothy, some clients came wanting to go home, to find safe, less conflicted, and more loving relationships. This is called Relational Therapy. The four main characters discovered that by working together each could achieve their own goals. This is called Group Therapy. Many came into therapy seeking a Great and Powerful Wizard, a therapist to magically "fix" them. My job, as a therapist was to help them all discover those creative hidden potentials within themselves. In the end, and if they completed their work, I hoped that they would discover that "I'm really a very good man, though I'm a very I'm a very bad Wizard." The real wizard was found within themselves, the wizard of us.

What can we, as magicians, learn from these five characters? How can we discover and develop our creative potentials-- the deeper knowing that is within every one of us? Are we always looking for that wizard, that one trick, DVD, book, lecture or convention that will magically make us a better magician? Maybe we already have what we need. Can we bring the color of Oz to the drabness to our "Kansas" magic? Do we need to *rethink* our magic presentations, our character, and our interactions with the audience? Do we need to express our *emotions* more in our presentations? What feelings do we now stir up in our audience members? What is the range of emotions that we want our audiences to experience? Do we have *courage* as we perform? What are our Flying Monkeys? Do we need to take more risks in our presentations? How do we act when a trick goes wrong? Do we blame the audience if we don't get the response we want? Are we so focused on our props and techniques that we fail to establish a relationship with the audience? How do we treat our volunteers? Do they feel safe as they assist us or are they afraid that we will make a fool of them? Do we allow our audiences to experience *our humanity*? Are we afraid of being vulnerable? Do we risk working with a director or safe group of magicians to improve our magic? We may be like the gate keeper to the Emerald City who says to the four pilgrims when they requested an audience with the Wizard, "Nobody gets in to see the wizard! Not nobody! Not no how!" Eugene Burger says it best, "Magic is about life not the props. Great magic is also about the magician."

Till next time, remember to cut the cards.

Performance Piece 2

Deeper Mystery Egg Bag

Background

On November 17, 1969, I fell in love with the Egg Bag. It was at a Charlie Miller lecture in the Dallas/Fort Worth area when I was in graduate school. Unlike the poorly made red woolen bag and wooden egg I got as a teen, Charlie had a Malini Egg Bag and used a real "blown" egg. In Charlie's hands I saw why the Egg Bag has been a long-time classic in magic. I quickly ordered the Charlie Miller Malini Egg Bag and excellent plastic egg from Magic, Inc. Since that time I have gotten several other Malini bags but am currently using Lynetta Welch's handcrafted black silk "Legacy Malini Egg Bag," which was "created by Max Malini, improved by Charlie Miller, and perfected by Johnny Thompson."

Mike, Johnny Thompson and the Egg Bag

The primary resources (bags, notes, books and DVDs) that I have drawn on for my handling the Egg Bag are Max Malini, Charlie Miller, Ken Brooks, Bob White, and Johnny Thompson. Some secondary sources have been Dan Tong, Jeff Hobson, Luis de Matos, and Martin Lewis. An excellent overview of various kinds of Egg Bags is John Novak's *The Egg Bag Book* published in 1999 by Stevens Magic Emporium.

The Egg Bag has rich history going back to the 1600s. Hocus Pocus Junior has a wood cut of Isaac Fawkes (1675-1731) performing with a very large bag, a number of eggs and a hen as the final load. The smaller bags that are used today are attributed to Herbert A. Albini (1860-1922) in 1891. It is believed that Max Malini (1873-1942) met Albini some years later. Scores of magicians have featured the Egg Bag in their acts for the past two hundred years.

Theory

I like the Egg Bag because it easily fits in my jacket pocket and can be used for close-up, stand-up and stage venues. The effect is very visual, the plot is simple, and can be used with music or a script. With good audience management skills the props can be briefly inspected. The main weaknesses I see is that some performers do too many vanishes and reappearances of the egg. I find that once or twice is enough for most audiences. Some performers spend too much time showing that the bag is not gimmicked. I turn the bag inside out once and let an audience member put their hand into the bag with the back of their hand touching the pocket side of the bag, making it difficult for them to feel the pocket. My experience is that for most audiences that is enough. I want the focus to be on the egg and not the bag as Al Baker used to say. Don't run if you aren't being chased!

The main theatrical challenge of the Egg Bag for the performer is how to end the routine with a punch. Past performers have produced livestock as an ending but that is impractical for most performers today. Luis de Matos produces a live chick from the bag in his stage show. Other performers have produced comedy items (i.e., rubber livestock, golf club, glass of liquid, etc.) I am proud of the ending I have created and use in my stand-up and stage shows. Basically, I end by breaking the egg into a small white dish to reveal a black "baby bag" after posing the question of which came first, "the egg or the bag?" This is a play on the old question of "which came first, the chicken or the egg?" Read the script below, and it will be clearer. Some of my magician friends have suggested that I put a tiny egg (a white Tic-Tac) inside the baby bag and have another punch for an ending. I have found that it is stronger for lay audiences to end with the baby bag. My close-up routine does not end with the breaking of the egg.

Egg Preparation

Because the preparation of the egg is labor intensive, I usually prepare a dozen "blown" eggs at one time. I make a dime to nickel size hole in one end of the egg. I start with puncturing one end of the egg with a large needle and then enlarge the hole with a small nail, then with a larger nail. I then use tweezers to carefully break the hole wider to the desired diameter. I remove the entire contents of the egg with a baby syringe and water over the sink. When the egg is completely empty, I wash it out and let it dry. I then insert a rolled-up tiny bag into the egg. My tiny bags (2 ½ inches square) were sewn by my wife from a thin fabric which matches the color of my black Malini Egg Bag. I then glue with Elmer's Glue two layers of torn white quarter size tissue paper over the hole. I do one layer and allow it to dry and then add the second layer. The torn glued tissue paper blends in with the surface of the egg better than cut circles of tissue. I let the eggs dry overnight. The glued tissue acts as a bridge for a thin layer of interior DAP Vinyl Spackling paste that I spread on top. I smooth the spackling paste using my wet fingers. After the spackling has dried, I then use a very fine sandpaper to finish the egg preparation. I store my eggs in a plastic egg container that can be purchased from a camping supply store.

Script

The following script is one that I wrote and was edited by Larry Hass. It fits my personality, character, and style of magic.

"As a magician I love learning about the history of magic. This next piece is one of the classics of the art. It is called the Egg Bag. The routine goes back to medieval times, when magicians would perform in the streets and at fairs.

In those days people didn't pay the performers with money. They paid them, instead, with things form the farm: vegetables, honey, milk, and . . . eggs! Would you hold this, please? Look inside: the bag is empty, yes? Put your hand inside to feel that it is empty. Yes? Now, drop the egg into the bag. Can

YOU see the egg? You, too? Now, can you feel the egg through the cloth? You, too? Yes? Three people have seen the egg; three people have FELT the egg. (Name), do you have a magic word? What is it?

Good, now wave your hand over the bag and say your special magic word. You did it! The egg is gone! Look into the bag! (Repeat) Feel inside the bag! (Repeat) Now wave your hand, and I'll say MY magic word: "Ker plunk!!" Reach inside and remove what you find.

Ladies and gentlemen, the mystery of the egg and the bag! But, wait! We are left with another question, a variation on the old conundrum: which came first, the bag or the egg? It seems obvious: the egg! But the mystery is deeper than you think. (Break the egg, revealing the small bag) A baby BAG!!!"

Part III: Gift Receiving and Giving

D. Michael Smith

20

Cynicism and Magic

In Bruce Springsteen's song "Magic" from his album *Magic* we find the following lyrics:
Trust none of what you hear
And less of what you see.
. . . So leave everything you know.
Carry what you fear. . . .
This is what will be, this is what will be.

In his song he refers to the props of magic: a coin, a card, rabbit in a hat, shackles, chain, and a shiny saw blade as metaphors for the ways the government, business, and other institutions of our culture "trick" us, distort the truth, lie, betray, and so on. This song came out in 2008, as the economic markets collapsed, Congress and the political processes were gridlocked, and the wars in the Middle East were still being fought. The whole album conveys a general sense of foreboding. It is not really about magic but about tricks.

Currently, we live in a culture that has become even more cynical than in many previous generations. With all respect to the "Boss," I believe that our culture needs more "magic," the kind we practice, to counter some of growing cynicism in our culture. First, a definition: Cynicism is a state of mind characterized by a general distrust of others' intentions, motives, and actions. It is the generalized lack of faith in others. Its philosophical source is the Cynics, an ancient Greek school of philosophers who denounced the conventional methods of seeking happiness (possessions, family, religion, etc.). Diogenes of Snope (412-323 B.C.), also known as "Diogenes the Cynic,' was the best known cynic.

So, how can our magic help us deal with cynicism? I believe magic, like good theater, asks us to "suspend our disbelief." Perhaps David Mamet, the screen and playwright and producer/director of magician Ricky Jay's Broadway shows, says it best:

> Now of course the magician didn't make that duck disappear. What he did was something of much greater worth—he gave a moment of joy and astonishment to some who were delighted by it.
>
> In suspending their disbelief—in suspending their reason, if you will—for a moment, the viewers were rewarded. They committed an act of faith, or of submission. And like those who rise refreshed from prayers, their prayers were answered. For the purpose of prayer was not, finally, to bring about intercession in the material world, but to lay down, for a time of the prayer, one's confusion and rage and sorrow at one's own powerlessness.
>
> So the purpose of the theater is not to fix the social fabric, not to incite the less perceptive to wake up and smell the coffee, not to preach to the converted about the delights (or burdens) of middle-class life. The purpose of theater, like magic, like religion—those three harness mates—is to inspire cleansing awe. (*Three Uses of the Knife: On the Nature and Purpose of Drama*, 1998, pp. 68-69)

So, do you see the irony? Our magic, our deceptions, can help deal with the cynicism of our audiences by helping them lay down, for a moment, their confusion, rage and sorrow and to be inspired by the "cleansing awe" of joy, wonder, surprise and delight. So, *STOP CYNICISM, DO MORE MAGIC!!*

Till next time, remember to cut the cards.

21

"Tis the Season"

Before retiring I was a marriage and family therapist working in a counseling center in Dallas, Texas. This piece is an adaptation from an unknown source written by Fletcher W. Swink. I first wrote it for the December 2012 Dallas Magic Clubs' *Wizards Scroll*. It was reprinted in the December, 2013 issue of the Society of American Magician's *M-U-M* and also in the Fort Worth Magicians Club *FlashPaper*. It has also been re-written and presented as a theatrical dialogue in a Theatre Arlington holiday production. Hope you enjoy it.

"Some years ago, when I was in the counseling center late one December night, a long distant phone call came in from a kindly old man asking if we were the best counseling center in Texas. I said that I thought we were. He then asked if I were little Sigie Freud. I said no, that I was little "Mikie" Smith. I said that I did have a beard and had smoked a cigar a time or two. I explained that the operator had connected him to a wrong number and that his timing was off by about 100 years. He apologized saying that where he lived, the days and nights are six months long so he often loses track of time.

I explained that I was a counselor and asked if I could help him. He would not make an appointment, saying that he lives too far away. When I suggested that he seek a therapist in his home town, he revealed that nobody lives there except him and his wife, a herd of reindeer, and a work crew of elves. He also said that he only gets away once a year and that is a flying trip that allows no time to stop for counseling. So, he wanted counseling over the phone.

"Well," I said, understandingly, "I can see why you would want to talk with someone. All those elves and reindeer could drive anyone crazy after a while."

"Oh, no!" he answered, "You don't understand. Life is great up here. I like my reindeer. I don't even mind being knee-deep in elves. What's driving me out of my mind is the crazy stuff people are saying about me."

"Oh no," I thought. "Is he getting senile or paranoid and having delusions of persecution? If old Kris Kringle goes off his rocker, what is left to believe in?"

"They are telling lies about me to their kids," he continued. "They have been telling them that I only bring goodies to children who behave like angels. I know why they do it. Some of them just aren't very bright and keep repeating the same nonsense they grew up with. But some of them do it to blackmail their kids into behaving. "Be good," they say, "or Santa won't bring you anything. Just look at what they are doing to me. Instead of a kindly old soul who really loves kids, they are making me look like some kind of dirty old man who goes around bribing kids to be good. I do it because I love them. Why can't those parents understand that? It looks like they just don't know much about love . . . or about kids either, for that matter." His voice seemed to grow a bit more calm and reflective. "Then again, maybe those parents aren't really trying to do me in. Maybe they can't teach much about love because they never learned much about it. I guess that's one of the reasons your counseling center exists- to help parents and kids understand more about love. I think it's sort of like what religious types call 'grace.' If they ever get that message, maybe they'll see that I don't deliver goodies because their kids are good. I do it because I am good."

He sighed deeply, as if glad to get something off his chest. Then he said, "Well, it's been good talking to you, Sonny. I really appreciate all the help you have given me. Now, how much do I owe you?"

"Well," I replied, "considering that yours is a rather unusual case, we'll let this one "be on the house." But, I do have one request and one question."

"What's that, Sonny?" he said resuming his former jovial tone.

I explained that I was also a magician and said, "I would like your permission to tell all my magician friends about this conversation." "You got it!! You magicians understand this season is really magical and wonder-filled. So, by all means! What's your question?"

"What are you going to bring me for Christmas, Santa?"

My hope is that this holiday season we truly believe that our "magic" can bring joy and wonder into people's lives.

Till next time, remember to cut the cards.

22

Magic is Good Medicine
Part 1

"Because I believe in transformation and empowerment, I never tire of sharing
what medicine and magic can say to each other."
Ricardo T. Rosenkranz, M.D.

In the next two chapters I want to explore the relationship between magic and
medicine. I am indebted to Jeff McBride for the phrase, "Magic Is Good
Medicine." He used it as a sign-off phrase in his *MAGIC Magazine* columns,
"Ask the Show Doctor," and in his book, *The Show Doctor* (2012). As you
know I am not a physician (in fact, I struggled with the sciences in school).
But, before retirement as a psychiatric hospital chaplain and mental health
therapist, I frequently consulted professionally with physicians.

Dallas's own Reade Quinton—physician, medical examiner, and educator—
recently attended the McBride School of Magic & Mystery conference on
"Magic and Medicine." In next chapter I will share some of his thoughts and
experiences from this conference that he described as the "best magic
conference and the best medical conference I've ever attended."

First, I want to explore some examples of the relationship between medicine
and magic. Ricardo Rosenkranz, M.D., professor medicine at Northwestern
School of Medicine in Chicago is also a magician. He teaches a course on
"Magic and Medicine" for medical students and says, "Magic and medicine
share the same DNA. Medicine is a performance art." In other words, magic
is in medicine; and medicine is in magic. Dr. Rosenkranz was one of the main
presenters at the annual McBride "Magic and Medicine" conference that Reade
attended. (See the article about Dr. Rosenkranz, "Healing Medicine through
Magic" in the April, 2014 issue of *MAGIC Magazine*.)

Another medical doctor has some notions about the magic in medicine and the medicine in magic. Paul A. Offit, M.D. in his book, *Do You Believe in Magic? The Sense and Nonsense of Alternative Medicine* (2013) quotes Art Caplan, professor of New York University's Langone Medical Center, in addressing the ethics of deception in the "placebo effect." He says it's ethical to deceive the patient at low risk, at low cost, and at low burden. "In fairness, all practitioners— mainstream or otherwise— employ some form of deception. They know that a positive attitude, reassuring demeanor, and air of competence are important. We use the placebo effect all the time." Offit continues, "From the days of shamans and witch doctors to the modern day physician, everybody has their props, their deceptions."

Still another example of the healing power of magic is from Norman Cousins (1915-1990), journalist, professor and author of *Anatomy of an Illness* (1979). Cousins once met with Albert Schweitzer (1875-1965), famous theologian, organist, philosopher, and medical missionary to Africa. Cousins wrote, "I had ventured the remark that local people were lucky to have access to the Schweitzer clinic instead of having to depend on witch-doctor supernaturalism. Dr. Schweitzer asked me how much I knew about witch doctors. I was trapped in my ignorance." The next day Schweitzer took Cousins into the jungle and introduced him to the local witch-doctor.

"For the next two hours, we stood off to one side and watched," reported Cousins. "With some patients, the witch doctor merely put herbs in a brown paper bag and instructed the ill person in their use. With other patients, he gave no herbs but filled the air with incantations. A third category of patients he merely spoke to in a subdued voice and pointed to Dr. Schweitzer." Later Schweitzer interpreted what they had seen. The first group had minor illness that would resolve on their own or with a little help. The second group had psychological problems and was treated with "African psychotherapy." The third group had more serious diseases the witch-doctor couldn't treat, so he directed them to see Dr. Schweitzer. "The witch doctor succeeds for the same reason the rest of us succeed," he said. "Each patient carries his own doctor inside him. They come to us not knowing that truth. We are at our best when we give the doctor who resides within each patient a chance to go to work."

Till next time, remember to cut the cards.

23

Magic Is Good Medicine
Part 2

In the last chapter I gave a quick overview of the relationship between magic and medicine. In this chapter we will hear from DMC's own Reade Quinton, M.D., regarding his participation in the McBride Magic & Mystery School conference "Magic and Medicine" in Las Vegas. Reade summarized his experience at the conference with these words: "This was the best magic conference and the best medical conference I've ever attended."

Consider these words in light of Reade's professional background in medicine and in magic. Until recently he was Deputy Chief Medical Examiner for Dallas County; Associate Professor of Pathology for the University of Texas Southwestern Medical School in Dallas where he also served as Director of Forensic Pathology Fellowship Programs. Currently Reade is a pathologist and a Professor at the famed Mayo Clinic in Rochester, Minnesota. At age nine Reade was exposed to magic at Disney World where he bought a Svengali deck. Later, after medical school, when he was doing a rotation in pediatrics, Reade rediscovered magic (Scotch and Soda and a few minor effects). When he moved to Dallas in 1999 to do a residency at UT Southwestern Medical School he visited Dallas area magic shop, Magicland, bought *Card College 1*, and attended his first magic lecture–Lennart Green. He joined the Dallas Magic Clubs in 2005 and attended his first magic convention, the 2006 Texas Association of Magicians Convention in Dallas. He is a member of both the IBM and SAM and has served as an officer in the Dallas Magic Clubs for five years. He entertains friends and family with his close-up magic and has worked with both the abused children and the counselors of the Dallas Children's Advocacy Center's summer and spring camps.

The fifteen participants in the Magic and Medicine Seminar included doctors, nurses, dentists, a medical student, hospital chaplain, a social worker, and an acupuncturist. The medical student that attended was there on a scholarship from his medical school. The presenters were all faculty members of the School of Magic Mystery that included Richardo Rosenkranz, M.D., Larry Hass, Ph.D., Eugene Burger, and Jeff McBride. Sessions each day included lectures, performances, experiential learning, time to visit Jeff's library and session times with the teachers and other students.

Reade said that one of his surprise lessons from the experience was that he broadened his definition of medicine and healing. He is a scientist and had approached medicine as being science, but this seminar let him experience medicine as a performance art and himself as an artist. He came to see that medicine and magic a have a shared DNA and that his magic is medicine and his medicine is magic.

Most participants focused their attention on using the magical arts as part of their "bedside manner" relationships with patients, especially children. Reade, a medical examiner, who "works with dead people," uses his bedside manner when he gives court testimony regarding his medical examination of the deceased person. He uses Max Maven's three questions that audiences ask of all performers: Who is this guy? What is he doing? And, why should I care? In the courtroom Reade's "audience" are the jury, judge, and the attorneys. Reade hopes to return to the seminar in a few years after he has had to digest all that he has learned and experienced.

Till next time, remember to cut the cards.

24

Breaking Our Magic Wands

"But this rough magic I here abjure, and when I have required some heavenly music, which even now I do, to work mine end upon their senses that airy charm is for, I'll break my staff, bury it certain fathoms in the earth, and deeper than did ever plummet sound I'll drown my book."
Prospero, *The Tempest*, Act 5, Scene 1

I begin with a quote from Robert E. Neale, "My current project is writing another book. I have taken the theme from Shakespeare's Prospero, that old magician who breaks his wand while still alive. What if I, and the other magicians I know, did the same: break our wands while still alive? What might that look like? What would it mean?" (*The Sense of Wonder*, p. 34). Neale's new book, *Breaking Our Magic Wands,* was released at the Magic and Meaning Conference in 2017.

Usually, we think of the "Broken Wand Ceremony" as occurring after a magician's death and conducted by one of the magic organizations. In light of Bob Neale's questions above, I want to suggest one way we can break our own wands while we are still alive. This comes from the experience I had with Geoff Grimes in helping Karen Heil dispose of her deceased husband's magic collection. Larry Heil, before his death by cancer in December, 2014, asked Geoff to dispose of his collection after his death. He wanted magicians to have his props, books, CDs, DVDs, etc. Geoff, in turn, asked me to help him since Larry had such a large collection.

One of the ways we can "break our own wands" while we are still alive is to make plans for dealing with our magic books, props, and so on. If we don't have a plan in place, the responsibility falls on our spouse, partner, or other family members to dispose of it. These folks often do not have a background, interest, or contacts in magic, and they often do not know the value of all our "magic junk." What follows are some concrete suggestions of what we can do before our death to help in the disposal of our magic.

1. While you are still living, regularly review your collection and give or sell what you want others to have.

2. Decide whether you intend your magic collection is to be primarily a source of financial income for the family or is it primarily a "gift" back to the magic community.

3. Designate a fellow magician who can assist your heirs with your magic collection. This person can help with selling your items either to one or two buyers of the whole collection or to individual buyers. Remember that some of relatives may want a few magic pieces as keep-sakes.

4. Indicate if you want your items to be auctioned at one of the several local or state-wide magic auctions. Some items can be sold on Ebay or on one of the online magic selling sites. Consult with magic collectors and dealers who can assist you.

5. Most of our dealer-acquired magic collections are not what auction houses (such as Potter & Potter Auctions) are looking to acquire. They are looking for very old, rare, or historically significant items.

6. Organize your collection in plastic bags with the instructions sheets and DVDs with the props or clearly organized in a separate location.

7. Clearly mark any collector's items and valuable out-of-print books.

Remember, our magic is a gift that we have received and it needs to be shared with others while we are living and after we are gone.

Till next time, remember to cut the cards.

25

Gifts from Eugene Burger

Eugene Burger died at age seventy-eight on August 8, 2017. Like most of you, I was shocked when I heard the news from Larry Hass. I remembered that some of us had been with Eugene at the end of April of the same year. It was at Main Street Magic in McKinney, Texas for the Hass farewell party from Texas to Tennessee. Eugene did a magic lecture the next day. Geoff Grimes and I had the privilege of picking up Eugene at the airport and driving him to the party site in McKinney. Because it was during the Friday afternoon rush hour we had more time in the car to visit with him. We cherish that time we had to talk about magic and about life. In his lecture he chose me to assist him in his magic effect, "Destiny Has a Name," in which my selected card also had my name printed on the back with his signature. That card, a gift from Eugene, is proudly displayed on my den book shelf.

In the weeks since learning of his death I reread some of his books and reviewed some of his DVDs and read his last book, co-authored with Larry Hass, *Teaching Magic: A Book for Students and Teachers of the Art*. My all-time favorite Burger book is *The Experience of Magic*, 1989. When I mentioned this to him he said it was his favorite book. My favorite Burger DVD is *Penguin Live Online Lecture: Eugene Burger,* 2015. Larry Hass has recently published the first of two books of Eugene's unpublished material entitled *Eugene Burger: From Beyond* (2019) with the second, *Eugene Burger: Final Secrets* planned for 2021.

Below are some lessons I learned from Eugene in his lectures, books, and DVDs:

- "My goal is to teach you to be a better magician not just to teach you tricks, but teach you how to perform them in ways that will create the impact (power, value, importance) you want."

- "The goal of the teacher is to produce students who are better than the teacher."

- "Magic is an art. Treat it that way."

- "There are many rooms in the House of Magic and every room demands a price."

- "Magic is about life not the props. Great magic is also about the magician."

- "One of the problems with magic is that magicians are afraid to be vulnerable. We need to know our character (who we are). It takes courage."

- "Your audience will never think your magic is more important (valuable) than you think it is."

- "A good magic trick is a trick that tomorrow morning the audience member can tell their neighbor what happened."

- "Magic tricks need a frame. *I deeply believe in scripts.* Every good magic trick deserves a good opening line and a good closing line."

- "A good magic show needs texture."

- "There is fabulous magic at every skill level and the challenge is to find it. If you stay with your skill level you can be a star."

- What are your criteria for selecting your magic? Avoid the tyranny of the new.

- A good magic effect should create the following in the minds of the audience members, "That was fair . . . that was fair . . . and that was fair . . . and yes, that was fair. Whoah! No freaking way!!!"

- "There is a difference between practice and rehearsal."

- "Our society needs more magic so that we can get bigger dreams."

- Eugene was fond of quoting philosopher, Alan Watts, especially his saying, "When you get the message, hang up the phone."

- "The enchantments of magic point beyond mere illusion to the Great Mystery of life, the eternal transformation of life, death, and rebirth."

I will end this with a quote from his obituary, written by his student, friend, and colleague, Larry Hass. "As Eugene said many times, magic is about life. And he showed us over and over with a simple strand of thread he was at peace with the fact of death—the great mystery." (*Genii: The Conjurors' Magazine*, Oct. 2017, p. 86)

Till next time, remember to cut the cards.

Eugene Burger and Mike

26

Gift Giving and Receiving

"They (the Magi) opened their treasures and offered him gifts." (Matthew 2:11)

The holidays are the season of gift giving and receiving. All the world cultures and religions emphasize some form of gift giving. Have you ever wondered about our universal need to give and receive gifts? Do you consider magic to be a gift you have and that needs to be given to others? I hope so. I want to explore gift giving a bit more in this column. To do this I want to refer you to two very helpful books (I consider books to be gifts): *The Gift: Creativity and the Artist in the Modern World* by Lewis Hyde, 1979, 2007; and *Gift Magic: Performances that Leave People with a Souvenir* edited by Lawrence Hass, 2010.

Lewis Hyde is also author of *Trickster Makes This World: Mischief, Myth, and Art*, 1998. The main point *The Gift* is that we need to understand that we live in the midst of two economies—"market economy" and "gift economy." Market economy is about buying and selling, producing things (commodities), and making money. This is the economy most of us are most familiar with.

But we also live in another economy—gift economy. Gift economy is about giving and receiving, about generating relationships and connections, about making community, and about inspiring worth and health. The main point Hyde is making is that gift economy is equally real, present and important in our lives. He is not saying that the market economy is unreal, false or unimportant. But they are different, related but irreducible. Deep problems come when we confuse the two or fail to recognize the gift economy, which happens a lot in American culture. Some art collectors buy art because it is a good investment (market) and some art collectors buy art because they love the artwork itself (gift).

Let's hear Hyde's own words: "It is the assumption of this book that a work of art is a gift, not a commodity. Or, to state the modern case with more precision, that works of art exist simultaneously in two 'economies,' a market economy and a gift economy. Only one of these is essential, however: a work of art can survive without the market, but where there is no gift there is no art."

Now let's hear from Larry Hass, who builds upon Hyde's work. "As we know from our experiences as artists, artwork is inspired and created. Indeed, art is not 'manufactured' or 'produced' like cars on an assembly line; that is the way the market produces commodities. On the contrary, art flows from inspiration and the flow itself is a creative one. Inspiration and creativity: these are things one only gets from the gift economy."

When I was a marriage and family therapist, a few people would say that my clients were buying my love and attention. This is a market economy perspective. My response was, "No, my love and attention are free gifts. The fee is to pay for my time." This is both gift economy and market economy.

When we do magic for others, we may or may not be paid for our time. The magic we do for others is the gift that flows from our inspiration and our creativity. May we share our inspiration and creativity in this world that needs a lot more magic! Happy Holidays and see you in the New Year!!

Till next time, remember to cut the cards.

27

The Art of Breaking Boxes

In the March 2018 issue of *M-U-M* (the monthly publication of the Society of American Magicians) John Shryock reports that when he does a magic show he begins with producing birds, lighted matches, candles and silks. "I like to show skill before going into boxes," he says. "Otherwise people can think, 'if I had that box, I could do that, too.'" That comment and my recent re-reading *of Amaze: the Art of Creating Magical Experiences* by Ferdinando Buscema and Mariano Tomatis got me thinking, not about "tricky boxes" or doing "big box" stage illusions, but about magic and boxes in general.

Buscema and Tomatis, two Italian magicians, in explaining their approach to breaking out of the traditional magic box say, "Exploring the subject, we realized we had in mind something different and more radical: we started to question the theatrical dimension of magic, because that setting seemed to be only one of many possibilities. We could think of many examples of 'magical experiences' drawn from everyday life, completely unrelated to the world of the illusionists: from the tears triggered by watching a movie to the adrenaline rush from playing an engaging game. Human existence was studded with stimuli artfully designed to amaze, paralyze, move and shake us. . . . It was time to write its manifesto. We chose as a title its highest goal: AMAZE."

As humans we grow up learning to put all our experiences into "boxes." When we are born we are completely empty. But as we grow, we quickly learn so many things: who we are; who we should and should not be; our family, race, gender, religion, education, region, nationality, political persuasion, etc. To help keep track of these learnings and to not get too emotionally overwhelmed, we put all our new facts and experiences into "boxes" so that we can easily recover them when needed. As we move into adulthood, these boxes become our "world view." We all have a world view whether we are aware of it or not. Much of the polarity we see in our culture today is due to our assumptions, our "boxes" that may or may not always be accurate. To really begin to understand each other, we need to hear and understand each other's' stories.

But sometimes things happen to us that we can't explain. We don't have a box to put it in. Magician Paul Harris, in his three DVDs, *The Art of Astonishment* says, "At that moment of trying to box the unboxable your world view breaks up." Harris calculates that the typical moment of awe and wonderment experienced by the average magic audience member lasts about ten seconds. After that period of time they instinctively start putting that experience into a "box." We all have heard some of these boxes: "it went up your sleeve box;" "it is done with a mirror box;" "I don't how you did it but it's a trick box;" and (back to John Shryrock); "if I had that box, I could do that, too box." And it really doesn't matter whether their boxes are correct or not. To them, it only matters that they have now put that experience into a "box." Their anxiety goes down and they can stop thinking.

I agree with Eric Mead when he says that our job as magicians is to prolong the magical experience. He says, "If I can convince you that the feeling these 'tricks' evoke is rare and wonderful, you no longer want to figure the trick out like a puzzle. How it's done becomes irrelevant. Instead, you try to be amazed. And instead of 'fooling' you, I'm honestly trying to help."

I'll close with this wonderful quote from Sam Sharpe, magic philosopher, who considered amazement the highest goal for the modern magician. He said, "The underlying purpose of magic in its many aspects is not to deceive people but to encourage them to approach life and cosmos in a state of wonder."

Till next time, remember to cut the cards.

28

Imaginative Gift Giving

The holiday season, whatever your religious tradition may be, is a time of gift giving and receiving. In fact, gift giving is an ancient tradition found in all cultures and religious traditions since the beginning of recorded history. For Christians the tradition of gift giving and receiving is grounded in the gifts that the Magi brought to the Christ child. Hanukkah ("dedication") is second only to Passover as the most observed Jewish holiday and includes giving of money (gelt) or gifts. The word, "magi" is plural of "magus," and in Latin means "kings" or "wise men." Our word for "magic" comes from the same root word. It also imbedded in our words, image, imagine and imagination. All these words come from Middle English via old French and finally from Latin.

Robert Neale reminds us in *Gift Magic* (p.148) that "Magic is a gift." He continues by saying that "It can create the appreciation that things are not as they seem, and therefore, that something better is possible. This gift counters demoralization by offering new possibility and hope." Wow! This moves magic way beyond just doing silly tricks for light amusement and distraction. But he doesn't stop there. He goes on to say (p. 151), "gifts reveal something about the giver; reveal something about the giver's understanding of the receiver; gifts offer connection between giver and receiver; and especially, gifts prompt gift exchange which helps foster friendship and community. All this involves a host of feelings, thoughts, and behaviors, so any specific giving can be quite a fulsome piece of interchange. Magical gifts can do all this too." At this point we all need to take a deep breath and think about our imaginative gift giving and receiving.

My goal here is not to try to unpack all this for you but to remind you to bring a deep appreciation to your gift of magic, regardless of your style, character, or venue. When we perform, we offer people an experience, an experience of delight, surprise, wonder, enchantment, and mystery. As gifts, we can provide entertainment to various nonprofit charities at reduced or no charge. We can also offer our audiences small, physical gifts. What are some of our giveaways? Here are only a few: signed cards; paper hats; coins and small objects; wands; altered borrowed objects; origami pieces; and booklets of easy to do magic for very interested youngsters. Blackstone used to give away live bunnies in his stage show, and Geoff Grimes gives away stuffed bunnies and magic wands in his children/family shows.

We can also gift some of our money, magic tricks, books and DVDs to other magicians, especially beginning magicians who have limited resources or established magicians in need. A few years ago *The Linking Ring* published a list of "Ongoing Magic Benevolence Projects," in which there were thirty different sites listed, too long for me to list here. Let me mention three: (1) The IBM Magicians Support Fund; (2) the S.A.M. Magic Endowment Fund; and (3) the McBride Magic & Mystery School Scholarship.

The book, *Gift Magic*, by Jeff McBride, George Parker, Lawrence Hass, Eugene Burger, Rich Bloch, and Robert Neale, has recently gone out of print. However, as a gift, you can get a FREE PDF copy if you sign up for one of the several membership levels available at The McBride Magic & Mystery School at: http://virtual.magicalwisdom.com/members/signup.

Have a wonderful and magical holiday season.

Till next time, remember to cut the cards.

Performance Piece 3

A Whole Ball of Wax

This is my presentation of "Waxed, "Lonnie Chevrie's gypsy thread done with dental floss.

Background: I first learned of "Waxed" from the October, 1986 article, "Waxed," in *Genii* (p. 286) by Charles Greene. There Greene credits Lonnie Chevrie for creating the effect. It was published by Lonnie as "The No-cavities Guarantee" in the March, 2007 *M-U-M*, pp. 41-43. Lonnie has also revealed his handling in his lectures, and on a DVD, and as a download from Penguin Magic (www.penguinmagic.com).

Effect: This is a gypsy thread routine that uses waxed dental floss. The magician introduces a box of Johnson & Johnson waxed dental floss, breaks off and displays a piece about 5-6 inches long, and then asks five or six spectators to each break off a piece the same size. The spectators then gather their separate pieces together and one of them rolls them into a tight ball. Only then does the magician takes the ball and sticks it to the center of his piece. While he holds one end of his piece the spectator holds the other. When the spectator slowly pulls on the strand the floss is shown to be fully restored.

Preparation and Performance: Consult the above references to learn Lonnie's preparation and performance of "Waxed." Here I want to explain my differences in preparation and performance.

Begin by pulling out about two feet of floss. Do not break the floss. Fold the floss to find the center and beginning there roll the two strands together between your thumb and forefinger into a tight little ball. Continue to roll the ball tightly until there is about five inches left from one end to the other. Fold that piece over into the top of the container and close the lid. You are now ready to perform the effect.

When you begin the effect, open the lid and take out the piece, hiding the ball between your right thumb and forefinger, and break off the piece. This is held up to demonstrate the size you want the spectators to break off. I have five adult spectators do so and as they do I begin my script. I then ask them to pass their piece to one of the spectators I choose and have this person roll all their pieces together into a tight ball. Only then do I take the ball my left thumb and forefinger and pretend to stick it to the center of my piece. I reality I hide the spectators' ball between my left thumb and forefinger. I display the piece, holding the end of the stand with my thumb and forefinger (along with the other ball). I then have a spectator take and gently pull the other end, revealing a fully restored piece of floss. The last three lines of my script are said as this is done.

Script: "Sadly, we live in a world that is broken: broken hearts; broken promises; broken hopes and dreams; broken relationships; broken bodies; and broken bonds.

We wish there was not so much brokenness in our world. Our universal dream is a dream of peace, reunion, and wholeness. The greatest healing magic for all is the power of love."

Last Words

"The enchantments of magic point beyond mere illusion to the Great Mystery of life, death, and rebirth."

Eugene Burger
(1939-2017)

Appendix

Paul Pruyser's Three Worlds Perspective

As I mentioned in the Introduction, Robert Neale, in his writings* about illusions and make-belief, draws heavily upon the work of Paul Pruyser, especially his "Three Worlds" perspective. These three worlds are outlined in *The Play of the Imagination: Toward a Psychoanalysis of Culture*, International Universities Press Inc., 1983. Paul W. Pruyser, Ph.D. (1916-1987) was as clinical psychologist and psychoanalyst with the Menninger Foundation where he was a Clinical Professor and Director of the Interdisciplinary Studies Program. He was influenced by Sigmund Freud, William James, Rudolf Otto, and D. W. Winnicott.

Pruyser's major contributions were in psychological theories of religion and culture, as seen in his exploration of eleven basic characteristics of a person's three worlds: the *Autistic;* the *Illusionistic;* and the *Realistic.* *Autism* is a pervasive neuro-developmental condition which interferes with a person's ability to communicate and interact with others. *Illusionism* is the use of artistic techniques to create the illusion of reality especially in a work of art. *Realism* is the attitude or practice of accepting a situation as it is and then dealing with it accordingly.

Autistic	Illusionistic	Realistic
untutored fantasy	tutored fantasy	sense perception
omnipotent thinking	adventurous thinking	had undeniable facts
utter whimsicality	orderly imagination	logical connections
free association	inspired connections	logical connections
ineffable images	verbalized images	look-and-see referents
hallucinatory entities	imaginative entities	actual entities
or events	or events	or events
private needs	cultural needs	factual needs
symptoms	symbols	signs, indices

dreaming	playing	working
sterility	creativeness	resourcefulness
internal objects	transcendent objects	external objects

* Neale's references to Pruyser's Three Worlds:

The Magic Mirror, with David Parr, (2002, pp. 48- 50)

Magic Matters (2009, pp. 90- 92)

The Magic of Celebration Illusion, (2013, pp. 101- 109)

An Essay on Magic, (2015, pp. 126- 132)

Recommended Reading

Barrish, Seth. *An Actor's Companion*. New York: Theatre Communications Group, 2015.

Beckwith, Tobias. *Beyond Deception: The Theory and Technique of Creating Original Magic, Volume I.* Las Vegas: Nevada: Triple Muse Publications, 2007.

Burger, Eugene. *The Experience of Magic.* Kaufman and Greenberg, 1989.

Burger, Eugene and Robert E. Neale. *Magic and Meaning.* Seattle: Hermetic Press, 1995, expanded second edition, 2009.

Burger, Eugene. *Mastering the Art of Magic.* Washington, DC: Kaufman and Company, 2000.

Buscema, Ferdinando and Mariano Tomatis. *Amaze: The Art of Creating Magical Experiences*: Italy: Sperling & Kupfer, 2014.

Hass, Lawrence. *Eugene Burger: From Beyond.* Memphis: Theory and Art of Magic Press, 2019

Hass, Lawrence (editor). *Gift Magic: Performances that Leave People with a Souvenir.* Sherman, TX: Theory and Art of Magic Press, 2007.

Hass, Lawrence. *Inspirations: Performing Magic with Excellence.* Sherman, TX: Theory and Art of Magic Press, 2015.

Hass, Lawrence. *Life Magic: Ideas and Mysteries.* Memphis, TN: Theory and Art of Magic Press, 2018.

Hass, Lawrence. *Transformations: Creating Magic Out of Tricks.* Theory and Art of Magic Press, 2007.

Howard, Max. *Creating Theatrical Magic: A Study of* The War Wizard *and the Magician as Actor*: Sherman, TX: Theory and Art of Magic Press, 2014.

Kleon, Austin. *Steal Like an Artist: 10 Things Nobody Told You About Being Creative*. New York: Workman Publishing, 2012.

Kuhn, Gustav. *Experiencing the Impossible: The Science of Magic.* Cambridge, MA: The MIT Press, 2019.

Lamont, Peter and Jim Steinmeyer. *The Secret History of Magic: The True Story of the Deceptive Art.* New York: TarcherPerigee, 2018.

Macknik, Stephen L., and Susana Martinez-Conde. *Sleights of Mind: What the Neuroscience of Magic Reveals About Our Everyday Deceptions*. New York: Henry Holt and Company, 2010.

McBride, Jeff. *The Show Doctor: New Routines, Expert Advice, and Other Prescriptions for Better Magic.* Sherman, TX: Theory and Art of Magic Press, 2012.

Neale, Robert E. *An Essay on Magic.* Sherman, TX: Theory and Art of Magic Press, 2015.

Neale, Robert E. *The Magic of Celebrating Illusion.* Sherman, TX: Theory and Art of Magic Press, 2013.

Neale, Robert E. *The Sense of Wonder.* Sherman, TX: Theory and Art of Magic Press, 2014.

Parker, George. *Performing Magic with Impact*: *Practical Ideas and Professional Routines.* Memphis, TN: Theory and Art of Magic Press, 2018.

Parr, David. *Brain Food.* Seattle, WA: Hermetic Press, Inc., 1998.

Riese, Eberhard. *Foundations: The Art of Staging Magic.* Coesfeld, Germany: Sic!-Verlag Schenk & Sondermeyer, 2006.

Sankey, Jay. *Beyond Secrets.* Sankey Magic, 2003

Wonder, Tommy, and Stephen Minch. *The Books of Wonder. Volumes I and II.* Seattle, WA: Hermetic Press, 1996.

Zabrecky, Rob. *A, B, Z's of Magic.* Vanishing Inc. Magic, 2018.

About the Author

D. Michael Smith is a retired minister, marriage and family psychotherapist, and educator. He is also a life-long magician who at the age of eleven fell in love with the wonder and make-believe of magic after seeing Mark Wilson and Nani Darnell perform live in his East Texas hometown.

For over sixty years Mr. Smith has provided magic programs for churches, schools, community organizations, and restaurants. He has also used magic as a form of play therapy with children in his psychotherapy practice. Mike is a member of the Society of American Magicians, the International Brotherhood of Magicians (Order of Merlin), as well as the Texas Association of Magicians. He is also a regular participant in the "Magic and Meaning Conference" at the McBride Magic & Mystery School. He has served President of both the Fort Worth and Dallas magic clubs and continues to write his regular column, "Make Believe: Discovering and Creating Magical Experiences" for both newsletters.

Along with Geoff Grimes Mike regularly presents "The Magic of Perception" programs in college psychology classes at Mountain View College in Dallas, Texas. He is also an actor with a theatrical performance company at Theatre Arlington, Arlington, Texas.